Journal of a Solitude

Books by May Sarton

Journal
of a Solitude

By May Sarton

W · W · NORTON & COMPANY · INC · New York

Copyright © 1973 by May Sarton

FIRST EDITION

Library of Congress Cataloging in Publication Data
Sarton, May, 1912–
    Journal of a solitude.
    I. Title.
PS3537.A832J68   818'.5'203 [B]   72-13464
ISBN 0–393–07474–9

Published simultaneously in Canada
by George J. McLeod Limited, Toronto

For permission to quote from personal letters thanks are due to: Sister
Mary David, Mrs. Basil de Selincourt, Madame Eugenie Dubois, Madame
Pierre Hepp (Camille Mayran).
    Introduction by Humphry Trevelyan to *Truth and Fantasy* by Goethe.
Weidenfeld and Nicolson, Ltd. © 1949.
    "The Artificial Nigger" from *A Good Man Is Hard to Find and Other
Stories*, by Flannery O'Connor. © 1955, Harcourt, Brace Jovanovich, Inc.
(First published in 1953 by *The Kenyon Review*.)
    Journal d'un homme de 30 ans by F. Mauriac. Librairie Ernest Flam-
marion.
    Young Man Luther by Erik Erikson, W. W. Norton and Company, Inc.
© 1958.
    The Divine Milieu by Teilhard De Chardin, © 1960, Harper & Row,
Publishers, Inc.
    The Collected Works of C. G. Jung, ed. by G. Adler, M. Fordham, and
H. Read, trans. by R. F. C. Hull, Bollingen Series XX, vol. 8, *The Struc-
ture and Dynamics of the Psyche* (copyright © 1960, 1969 by Bollingen
Foundation); vol. 9i, *The Archetypes and the Collective Unconscious*
(copyright © 1959, 1969 by Bollingen Foundation); vol. 11, *Psychology
and Religion: West and East* (copyright © 1958, 1969 by Bollingen
Foundation); vol. 13, *Alchemical Studies* (copyright © 1967 by Bollingen
Foundation); vol. 14, *Mysterium Coniunctionis* (copyright © 1963 by
Bollingen Foundation), reprinted by permission of Princeton University
Press: short quotes from each volume.
    Le Mal et la Souffrance by Louis Lavelle, Librairie Plon, © 1940.
    The Collected Works of Paul Valery, ed. by Jackson Mathews, Bollingen
Series XLV, vol. 10, *History and Politics*, trans. by Jackson Mathews and
Denise Folliot (copyright © 1962 by Bollingen Foundation), reprinted
by permission of Princeton University Press: quote from p. 561.
    Clark E. Moustakas, *Loneliness*. © 1961. Reprinted by permission of
Prentice Hall, Inc., Englewood Cliffs, New Jersey.
    "Mist in the Valley" by Edna St. Vincent Millay, *Collected Poems*.
Harper & Row, Publishers, Inc. © 1928, 1955 by Edna St. Vincent Millay
and Norma Millay Ellis. By permission of Norma Millay Ellis.
    Haniel Long's poem "If Our Great Fragile Cities," from *The Grist
Mill*. © Rydal Press, Santa Fe, New Mexico, 1945.
    William Butler Yeats, "Nineteen Hundred and Nineteen" (stanzas 1, 2,
4), *Collected Poems*. © 1928. Permission granted by The Macmillan Com-
pany. Copyright renewed 1956 by Georgie Yeats.
    Claire Tomalin's review of LM's book from *New Statesman*, London. ©
July 2, 1972.
    James Kirkup, "The Poet," *A Spring Journey and Other Poems*. Oxford
University Press, © 1954.
    © 1957 *The New Yorker Magazine*, Inc. Reprinted from the book
A Poet's Alphabet by Louise Bogan. 1970. McGraw-Hill Book Company.
With permission of the publishers.
    "I Could Give All to Time" from *The Poetry of Robert Frost*, edited
by Edward Connery Lathem. Copyright 1942 by Robert Frost. Copyright
© 1970 by Lesley Frost Ballantine. Reprinted by permission of Holt, Rine-
hart and Winston, Inc.

PRINTED IN THE UNITED STATES OF AMERICA

1 2 3 4 5 6 7 8 9 0

FOR ERIC SWENSON

Journal of a Solitude

September 15th

BEGIN HERE. It is raining. I look out on the maple, where a few leaves have turned yellow, and listen to Punch, the parrot, talking to himself and to the rain ticking gently against the windows. I am here alone for the first time in weeks, to take up my "real" life again at last. That is what is strange—that friends, even passionate love, are not my real life unless there is time alone in which to explore and to discover what is happening or has happened. Without the interruptions, nourishing and maddening, this life would become arid. Yet I taste it fully only when I am alone here and "the house and I resume old conversations."

On my desk, small pink roses. Strange how often the autumn roses look sad, fade quickly, frost-browned at the edges! But these are lovely, bright, singing pink. On the mantel, in the Japanese jar, two sprays of white lilies, recurved, maroon pollen on the stamens, and a branch of peony leaves turned a strange pinkish-brown. It is an elegant bouquet; *shibui*, the Japanese would call it. When I am alone the flowers are really seen; I can pay attention to them. They are felt as presences. Without them I would die. Why do I say that? Partly because they change before my eyes. They live and die in a few days; they keep me closely in touch with process, with growth, and also with dying. I am floated on their moments.

The ambience here is order and beauty. That is what frightens me when I am first alone again. I feel inadequate. I have made an open place, a place for meditation. What if I cannot find myself inside it?

I think of these pages as a way of doing that. For a long time now, every meeting with another human being has been a collision. I feel too much, sense too much, am exhausted by the reverberations after even the simplest conversation. But the deep collision is and has been with my unregenerate, tormenting, and tormented self. I have written every poem, every novel, for the same purpose—to find out what I think, to know where I stand. I am unable to become what I see. I feel like an inadequate machine, a machine that breaks down at crucial moments, grinds to a dreadful halt, "won't go," or, even worse, explodes in some innocent person's face.

Plant Dreaming Deep has brought me many friends of the work (and also, harder to respond to, people who think they have found in me an intimate friend). But I have begun to realize that, without my own intention, that book gives a false view. The anguish of my life here—its rages—is hardly mentioned. Now I hope to break through into the rough rocky depths, to the matrix itself. There is violence there and anger never resolved. I live alone, perhaps for no good reason, for the reason that I am an impossible creature, set apart by a temperament I have never learned to use as it could be used, thrown off by a word, a glance, a rainy day, or one drink too many. My need to be alone is balanced against my fear of what will happen when suddenly I enter the huge empty silence if I cannot find support there. I go up to Heaven and down to Hell in an hour, and keep alive only by imposing upon myself inexorable routines. I write too many letters and too few poems. It may be outwardly silent here but in the back of my mind is a clamor of human voices, too many needs, hopes, fears. I hardly ever sit still without being haunted by the "undone" and the "unsent." I often feel exhausted, but it is not my work that tires (work is a rest); it is the effort of pushing away the lives and needs of others before I can come to the work with any freshness and zest.

September 17th

CRACKING OPEN the inner world again, writing even a couple of pages, threw me back into depression, not made easier by the weather, two gloomy days of darkness and rain. I was attacked by a storm of tears, those tears that appear to be related to frustration, to buried anger, and come upon me without warning. I woke yesterday so depressed that I did not get up till after eight.

I drove to Brattleboro to read poems at the new Unitarian church there in a state of dread and exhaustion. How to summon the vitality needed? I had made an arrangement of religious poems, going back to early books and forward into the new book not yet published. I suppose it went all right—at least it was not a disaster—but I felt (perhaps I am wrong) that the kind, intelligent people gathered in a big room looking out on pine trees did not really want to think about God, His absence (many of the poems speak of that) or His presence. Both are too frightening.

On the way back I stopped to see Perley Cole, my dear

old friend, who is dying, separated from his wife, and has just been moved from a Dickensian nursing home into what seems like a far better one. He grows more transparent every day, a skeleton or nearly. Clasping his hand, I fear to break a bone. Yet the only real communication between us now (he is very deaf) is a handclasp. I want to lift him in my arms and hold him like a baby. He is dying a terribly lonely death. Each time I see him he says, "It is rough" or "I did not think it would end like this."

Everywhere I look about this place I see his handiwork: the three small trees by a granite boulder that he pruned and trimmed so they pivot the whole meadow; the new shady border he dug out for me one of the last days he worked here; the pruned-out stone wall between my field and the church. The second field where he cut brush twice a year and cleared out to the stone wall is growing back to wilderness now. What is done here has to be done over and over and needs the dogged strength of a man like Perley. I could have never managed it alone. We cherished this piece of land together, and fought together to bring it to some semblance of order and beauty.

I like to think that this last effort of Perley's had a certain ease about it, a game compared to the hard work of his farming years, and a game where his expert knowledge and skill could be well used. How he enjoyed teasing me about my ignorance!

While he scythed and trimmed, I struggled in somewhat the same way at my desk here, and we were each aware of the companionship. We each looked forward to noon, when I could stop for the day and he sat on a high stool in the kitchen, drank a glass or two of sherry with me, said,

"Court's in session!" and then told me some tall tale he had been cogitating all morning.

It was a strange relationship, for he knew next to nothing about my life, really; yet below all the talk we recognized each other as the same kind. He enjoyed my anger as much as I enjoyed his. Perhaps that was part of it. Deep down there was understanding, not of the facts of our lives so much as of our essential natures. Even now in his hard, lonely end he has immense dignity. But I wish there were some way to make it easier. I leave him with bitter resentment against the circumstances of this death. "I know. But I do not approve. And I am not resigned."

In the mail a letter from a twelve-year-old child, enclosing poems, her mother having pushed her to ask my opinion. This child does really look at things, and I can write something helpful, I think. But it is troubling how many people expect applause, recognition, when they have not even begun to learn an art or a craft. Instant success is the order of the day; "I want it *now!*" I wonder whether this is not part of our corruption by machines. Machines do things very quickly and outside the natural rhythm of life, and we are indignant if a car doesn't start at the first try. So the few things that we still do, such as cooking (though there are TV dinners!), knitting, gardening, anything at all that cannot be hurried, have a very particular value.

September 18th

THE VALUE of solitude—one of its values—is, of course, that there is nothing to *cushion* against attacks from within, just as there is nothing to help balance at times of particular stress or depression. A few moments of desultory conversation with dear Arnold Miner, when he comes to take the trash, may calm an inner storm. But the storm, painful as it is, might have had some truth in it. So sometimes one has simply to endure a period of depression for what it may hold of illumination if one can live through it, attentive to what it exposes or demands.

The reasons for depression are not so interesting as the way one handles it, simply to stay alive. This morning I woke at four and lay awake for an hour or so in a bad state. It is raining again. I got up finally and went about the daily chores, waiting for the sense of doom to lift—and what did it was watering the house plants. Suddenly joy came back because I was fulfilling a simple need, a living one. Dusting never has this effect (and that may be why I am such a poor housekeeper!), but feeding the cats when they are hungry, giving Punch clean water, makes me suddenly feel calm and happy.

Whatever peace I know rests in the natural world, in feeling myself a part of it, even in a small way. Maybe the gaiety of the Warner family, their wisdom, comes from this, that they work close to nature all the time. As simple as that? But it is not simple. Their life requires patient understanding, imagination, the power to endure constant adversity—the weather, for example! To go with, not against the elements, an inexhaustible vitality summoned back each day to do the same tasks, to feed the animals, clean out barns and pens, keep that complex world alive.

September 19th

THE SUN is out. It rose through the mist, making the raindrops sparkle on the lawn. Now there is blue sky, warm air, and I have just created a wonder—two large autumn crocuses plus a small spray of pink single chrysanthemums and a piece of that silvery leaf (artemisia? arethusa?) whose name I forget in the Venetian glass in the cosy room. May they be benign presences toward this new day!

Neurotic depression is so boring because it is repetitive, literally a wheel that turns and turns. Yesterday I broke off from the wheel when I read a letter from Sister Mary David. She is now manager of a co-op in the small town in South Carolina where she has chosen to work. Always her letters bring me the shock of what is really going on and the recognition of what one single person can do. "So," says Sister Mary David, "I am of course mostly involved in the co-op work, but I do find more and more of the desperate families which are so numerous in this state—people who are frustrated, lonely, sick, helpless. One day I took an old man shopping. He was completely out of food and by some error his check had been stopped for three months. He bought what he needed and the bill came to $10.06. I emptied my wallet and what was in it came to *exactly* $10.06! So I suspect that the good Lord is at my elbow all the time. So many inexplicable things occur. Another day an elderly lady waited for me in the rain outside a second-hand furniture store to ask me to talk to a twelve-year-old boy who had tried to commit suicide. His father and stepmother had put him out—no clothes, no place to go. Well, he is better now. I bought him clothes and a folding bed which his old 'gran'ma' agreed to let him set up in her shack. I keep in touch, bought him a lunch box yesterday. They just seem to cross my path, dozens of them, and some disappear after the crisis."

I felt lifted up on the joy of sending a check and knowing that money would be changed at once into help. We are all fed up, God knows, with institutional charity, with three requests from the same organization in a week and often one to which a check had been mailed two weeks earlier. We are all, receivers and givers alike, computerized. It feels arid compared to the direct human way shown by Sister Mary David; she was not sent down by her order, but found her own way there on a summer project and then decided that she must stay, and somehow got permission to do so. This must be the tradition of the Sisters of Mercy.

The most hopeful sign, the only one, in these hard times is how much individual initiative manages to make its way up through the asphalt, so many tough shoots of human imagination. And I think at once of Dr. Gatch who started in Beaufort, South Carolina to heal sick blacks on his own. Whatever his tragic end, he did force the situation down there—near starvation—on the attention of Congress and the people of the United States. We have to believe that each person *counts*, counts as a creative force that can move mountains. The great thing Gene McCarthy did, of course, was to prove this on the political scene. While we worked for him we believed that politics might give way to the human voice. It is tragic that the human flaws can then wreck every-thing—McCarthy's vanity, Gatch's relying on drugs to keep going. We can do anything, or almost, but how balanced, magnanimous, and modest one has to be to do anything! And also how patient. It is as true in the arts as anywhere else.

So ... to work. It is not a *non sequitur*. I shall never be one of those directly active (except as a teacher, occasion-ally), but now and then I am made aware that my work, odd though it seems, does help people. But it is only in these last years at Nelson that I have known that for sure.

September 21st

YESTERDAY, SUNDAY, was Perley Cole's birthday. I went to see him in the afternoon and took him some pajamas. This time we were able to have a little talk. He is suffering from the change to a new place, although to an outsider this seems such an improvement on the horrible old one, that dirty old farmhouse sinking into the ground, and the atmosphere of lies there and of neglect, a place where more than one child has simply abandoned a senile parent, buried him alive. But Perley had put out roots there, had to, to keep his sense of himself. And now those roots have been torn away. How long can it last? His hands are transparent, and only his eyes, their piercing look that says so much more than he can utter, remain Perley Cole.

Yesterday before I left on the sad expedition I had looked out and seen two elderly people standing at the edge of the lawn, then walking down the hill a way and coming back, obviously in the hope I would come out. So I did. Apparently they have come more than once, lovers of *Plant Dreaming Deep* and of the poems. They turned out to be Charlotte and Albert Oppler, German refugees from Hitler, who landed here and later were sent to Japan under Mac-Arthur, Albert as a legal expert who helped draw up the new Japanese constitution. Of course, they know Elizabeth Vining, whose autobiography I am reviewing for the *Times* these days. But why did I tell them, nearly in tears, of my depression? It is quite absurd to tell total strangers such things. I suppose I was taken by surprise like an animal in a lair. I had been writing all morning, was open from the inside out, unprepared for kindness and understanding such as they showed. Here the inner person is the outer person. It is what I want, but that does not make me any less absurd.

Found this in an old journal of mine—Humphry Trevelyan on Goethe: "It seems that two qualities are necessary if a great artist is to remain creative to the end of a long life; he must on the one hand retain an abnormally keen awareness of life, he must never grow complacent, never be content with life, must always demand the impossible and when he cannot have it, must despair. The burden of the mystery must be with him day and night. He must be shaken by the naked truths that will not be comforted. This divine discontent, this disequilibrium, this state of inner tension is the source of artistic energy. Many lesser poets have it only in their youth; some even of the greatest lose it in middle life. Wordsworth lost the courage to despair and with it his poetic power. But more often the dynamic tensions are so powerful that they destroy the man before he reaches maturity."

Must art come from tension? A few months ago I was dreaming of a happy work, a whole book of poems stemming from fruitful love. Now here I am back on the rack. But perhaps this is a sign of health, not sickness. Who knows?

Perley Cole died last night. I saw him at three thirty, only half conscious, so I did not try to rouse him, just stood by the bed for a few moments. At six the matron at the nursing home telephoned to say he was failing, and when I called back an hour later told me he had gone to the hospital in Keene in an ambulance. (Why didn't they let him die there in the nursing home?) Mary, his youngest daughter, miles away in Charlestown, told me he died in the ambulance. There will be no service, a cremation, the body shipped *alone* to Cambridge for that, and the ashes will be strewn in the Hillsboro cemetery. He had been separated from his wife for years because of her long illness. It is the loneliest dying and the loneliest death I ever heard of. How many times he has said to me in these last months, "I never thought it would end like this."

How is one to accept such a death? What have we come to when people are shoveled away, as if that whole life of hard work, dignity, self-respect, could be discarded at the end like an old beer can?

He taught me a great deal. His slow steady way of working taught me patience—"Easy does it." His infinite care about small tasks, the way he knelt to clip around the trees after cutting the grass, the way he worked, not for me but to hold up his own standards of a good job—and he must have known very well that half the time I could not really appreciate what that "good job" had involved. I loved him, loved that streak of wildness in him that might make him lay down his tools and walk off, at war with some demon. He lived in a state of intense personal drama, and that, perhaps, is what lifted him out of the ordinary. Deep down we recognized each other long ago as of the same breed, passionate, ornery, and proud. I say it at the end of my poem about him, *A Recognition.** Let me remember that now, the man as he was:

> Now Perley says, "God damn it!"—and much worse.
> Hearing him, I get back some reverence.
> Could you, they ask, call such a man your friend?
> Yes (damn it!), and yes world without end!

* *A Private Mythology.*

Brancusi's game and his make the same sense,
And not unlike a prayer is Perley's curse.

So let the rest go, and heel down, my boy,
And praise the artist till Hell freezes over,
For he is rare, he with his scythe (no toy),
He with his perils, with his skill and joy,
Who comes to prune, to make clear, to uncover,
The old man, full of wisdom, in his prime.
There in the field, watching him as he passes,
I recognize that violent, gentle blood,
Impatient patience. I would if I could,
Call him my kin, there scything down the grasses,
Call him my good luck in a dirty time.

"That's the way it is," he used to say.

September 25th

YESTERDAY picked mushrooms on the front lawn, and a cup
of raspberries for Mildred. The leaves are falling fast, but so
far the colors are gentle, not the blaze of October yet. And
we are having tropical air, humid, depleting.

September 28th

THE SUN is out. I woke to lovely mists, dew on spider webs everywhere, although the asters look beaten down after the rain and the cosmos pretty well battered. But these days one begins to look up at the flowering of color in the leaves, so it is easier to bear that the garden flowers are going one by one.

Mildred is here cleaning. I think of all the years since she first began to come here and how her presence, so quiet, humorous, and distinguished, has blessed all that is here. The solitude is animated but not broken. I sit at my desk and work better because I know her sensitive hands are busy dusting and making order again. And when we sit down at ten for coffee and a talk, it is never small talk. Today she told me that she had seen a perfect round cobweb in the branches of the chokecherry outside her back window, sparkling with the dew on it. She and I have lived through a lot of joy and grief together and now they are "woven fine" through all that we exchange.

I am an ornery character, often hard to get along with. The things I cannot stand, that make me flare up like a cat making a fat tail, are pretentiousness, smugness, the coarse grain that often shows itself in a turn of phrase. I hate vulgarity, coarseness of soul. I hate small talk with a passionate hatred. Why? I suppose because any meeting with another human being is collision for me now. It is always expensive, and I will *not* waste my time. It is never a waste of time to be outdoors, and never a waste of time to lie down and rest even for a couple of hours. It is then that images float up and then that I plan my work. But it is a waste of time to see people who have only a social surface to show. I will make every effort to find out the real person, but if I can't, then I am upset and cross. Time wasted is poison.

That is why Nelson has been good for me, for my neighbors here are never pretentious, rarely smug, and their coarseness, where it exists, is rough and healthy. I could not be bored by the Warners, by Mildred, by Arnold Miner, just as the truly cultivated and sophisticated person (as rare as hens' teeth around here) never bores—I bask in Helen Milbank's rare visits. Best of all are the true intimates such as Anne Woodson, K. Martin, or Eleanor Blair, the old true friends with whom the conversation becomes a bouquet of shared joys and a shared vision of life. Eleanor has just been here for the weekend. We had a marvelous picnic, high up over the Connecticut valley in a field. We spread our blanket in the shade at the edge of woods, and spent a heavenly hour, absorbing the hazy gentle hills, the open space, the presence of the river with its nineteenth-century atmosphere. The whole scene might have been an engraving, because, I suppose, the river is not navigable, so even the bank has hardly changed in a hundred years. Near at hand we listened to many small chirring sounds of autumn insects, and on the way back Eleanor pointed out to me an amazing bright green, longwinged insect like a grasshopper. Further along she picked two branches of barberry rich in the red fruit, now lovely in the Japanese jar on the mantel here.

Nevertheless, getting ready for a guest and cooking meals

seemed an almost insuperable effort because I am so depressed. Depression eats away psychic energy in a dreadful way. But of course it did me good to make the effort. I stuffed an eggplant with ham and mushrooms, a dish new to Eleanor and very good; it looks so grand too, the wrinkled purple eggplant standing up in a bowl surrounded by sweet potatoes.

All this pleasure was marred at the end by my fatigue and exasperation at a small remark about flowers in a vase being faded, blowing off in a classic example of my irrational angers. I must have screamed terribly loudly as I have lost my voice today! The punishment fits the crime perfectly. I feel crippled, unable to speak, having uttered horrible things. These angers are crippling, like a fit when they happen, and then, when they are over, haunting me with remorse. Those who know me well and love me have come to accept them as part of me; yet I know they are unacceptable. I must try to solve them, to learn how to head them off, as an epileptic learns to head off an attack with medicine. I sometimes feel it is a Laocoön struggle between anger and my life itself, as if anger were a witch who has had me in her power since infancy, and either I conquer her or she conquers me once and for all through the suicidal depression that follows on such an exhibition of unregenerate behavior.

Sometimes I think the fits of rage are like a huge creative urge gone into reverse, something dammed up that spills over, not an accumulated frustration that must find a way out and blows off at some tiny irrelevant thing. I have had these fits since I was an infant; the story goes back to Womdelgem when I was two years old. On a rainy winter day I was taken out in my white fur coat and became fascinated by a bowl of goldfish in a shop window. I wanted it passion-

ately and when I was told "No," I flung myself, white coat
and all, into a mud puddle. The tantrums worried my parents and on medical advice they tried putting me, fully
clothed, into a tepid bath when it happened again. Next time
I screamed in my rage, "Put me in the bath! Put me in the
bath!" This suggests that at that age I was aware even while
in the tantrum that somehow it had to be controlled, that I
needed help, as we say these days.

But there is a difference between wanting something and
not being given it and the episode the other day. That
exploded from what I felt (irrationally) to be criticism of an
unjust kind. Tension had built up simply by my trying to
cope with the mundane side of having a guest. I had tried
hard to make it in every way a good time for Eleanor, old
and dear friend. And I felt in a quite idiotic way attacked.
Of course, I also take pride in the flower arrangements and
cannot bear having faded flowers around. But the reaction
was wildly out of proportion, and that was what made it
frightening. At such times I really feel as if my head were
going to burst and there is no doubt that the tantrum itself is
a release. But it is paid for very heavily in guilt and shame.
"Anger is a short madness," says Horace.

I have sometimes wondered also whether in people like
me who come to the boil fast (*soupe au lait*, the French call
this trait, like a milk soup that boils over) the tantrum is not
a built-in safety valve against madness or illness. My mother
buried her anger against my father and I saw the effects in
her of this restraint—migraine headaches and tachycardia, to
name only two. The nervous system is very mysterious. For
the very thing that made her an angry person also gave her
amazing strength with which to meet every kind of ordeal.

The anger was buried fire; the flame sustained my father and me through the hard years when we were refugees from Belgium and slowly finding our place in American life.

The fierce tension in me, when it is properly channeled, creates the good tension for work. But when it becomes unbalanced I am destructive. How to isolate that good tension is my problem these days. Or, put in another way, how to turn the heat down fast enough so the soup won't boil over!

September 29th

FROST WAS PREDICTED for last night, so I went out and gathered boughs of tomatoes, still green, and have hung them in the laundry room upstairs, hoping they may ripen there. Then I picked all the tender little flowers I could find—nasturtium, cosmos, a few bachelor's-buttons, a few late roses—and finally potted three begonias and red geraniums to bring into the house. The begonias have thrived remarkably, first as house plants last winter, then outdoors all summer. A sturdy plant is a great comfort. The light was sad, late in the afternoon, as I did these chores. So far this autumn has not been one of the glorious ones. Now this morning there is a thunderously dark overcast as Gracie Warner rakes leaves and cuts the grass one more time. I long for the bulbs to arrive, for the early autumn chores are melancholy, but the

planting of bulbs is the work of hope and always thrilling. I
shall be glad for October, when this queer, hot, uncertain
September has gone its way.

I have been playing the *Kindertoten lieder* for the first
time in years. I suppose it is a kind of symbolic gesture. I
have lost no children; it is the infant in myself who must
be forced to grow up, and in so doing to die to its infant
cries and rages. As I wrote that last sentence, I remembered
Louise Bogan's remarkable review of Caitlin Thomas's
Leftover Life to Kill. Louise says,

> Innocence and violence are terrible things. The severe
> rituals imposed on adolescents in practically every
> tribe known to anthropology insist on two basic dicta:
> grow up and calm down. In maturity, it is neces-
> sary, mankind has discovered, to suppress outbursts of
> strong emotion—joy, rage, grief—that may, in their irra-
> tionality, disturb the general peace. The Greeks came to
> fear those who threw themselves against the will of the
> gods. The grave choruses of the tragedies continually
> warn, caution, and seek to make reasonable the man or
> woman in the throes of whatever overweening passion;
> the gods are sure to punish such pride. Yet it is true,
> and always has been, that innocence of heart and vio-
> lence of feeling are necessary in any kind of superior
> achievement; the arts cannot exist without them. Cai-
> tlin Thomas here proves herself to be one of those rare
> individuals who have been able to keep hold of these
> dangerous qualities, in a pure state and to a highly
> operative degree, into the years when most people have
> lost them for good.

Yet Caitlin Thomas is not a great artist. Louise used to
say to me, "You keep the Hell out of your work." I have
thought much about this. I have felt that the work of art (I

am thinking especially of poetry), a kind of dialogue between me and God, must present resolution rather than conflict. The conflict is there, all right, but it is worked through by means of writing the poem. Angry prayers and screaming prayers are unfit for God's ears. So there is Hell in my life but I have kept it out of the work. Now it threatens to wreck what I care for most—to drive me back into a solitude that has, since I have been in love for a year and a half, ceased to be fruitful, become loneliness instead. And now I am trying to master the Hell in my life, to bring all the darkness into the light. It is time, high time, that I grew up.

"How does one grow up?" I asked a friend the other day. There was a slight pause; then she answered, "By thinking."

". . . *l'expérience du bonheur, la plus dangeureuse, par ce que tout le bonheur possible augmente notre soif et que la voix de l'amour fait retentir un vide, une solitude.*"*

October 5th

I WOKE to the meadow bright silver with frost, and brilliant sunlight through yellow leaves over the barn. What would I do without this calming open space to rest my eyes on? It is the mystical opening of the whole place. It is what I come

---

* ". . . the experience of happiness, the most dangerous, because all the happiness possible increases our thirst and the voice of love makes an emptiness, a solitude reverberate." François Mauriac, *Journal d'un Homme de 30 Ans.*

back to when I have been away, as to a deeper breath. Each time I am gone, even for a weekend, I have to recover the house and the garden; something dies with absence and must be reconstructed.

I met an avalanche of mail, some lovely surprises such as a huge puffball covered in herbs, with directions for cooking —a kind of magic object, for I have never seen one before. In another package I found a jar of homemade fig preserves. I felt the blessing in these presents, not bought, but hunted out or made by hand.

I managed to push all this aside, including thirty or so letters, because, as I drove home through the clear autumn light, all along the Connecticut river, meeting the hills as old companions as I neared Brattleboro, I was determined to make space, inner space for a poem. Loss made everything sharp. I suffer from these brief weekends, the tearing up of the roots of love, and from my own inability to behave better under the stress. The poem is about silence, that it is really only there that lovers can know what they know, and there what they know is deep, nourishing, nourishing to the palms of the hands and the soles of the feet. For a little while it is as if my nakedness were clothed in love. But then, when I come back, I shiver in my isolation, and must face again and try to tame the loneliness. The house is no friend when I walk in. Only Punch gives a welcoming scream; there are no flowers. A smell of stale tobacco, unopened windows, my life waiting for me somewhere, asking to be created again.

Among the other packages I found the first copies of *Kinds of Love*. I just glanced at it, saw that Norton had done a beautiful job with the jacket, then packed up three to go to friends. But it was awful that there was no one here to celebrate!

The autumn crocus is marvelous and the lavender asters, blue flames among the fallen leaves. I picked crocus for the Venetian glass on the mantel in the cozy room, and a few late roses. Then I cooked supper. The puffball was a terrifying mustardy green and tasted rather bitter.

I woke in tears this morning. I wonder whether it is possible at nearly sixty to change oneself radically. Can I learn to control resentment and hostility, the ambivalence, born somewhere far below the conscious level? If I cannot, I shall lose the person I love. There is nothing to be done but go ahead with life moment by moment and hour by hour—put out birdseed, tidy the rooms, try to create order and peace around me even if I cannot achieve it inside me. Now at ten thirty there is such radiant light outside that the house feels dark. I look through the hall into the cozy room, all in darkness, right through to the window at the end, and a transparent sheaf of golden and green leaves. And here in my study the sunlight is that autumn white, so clear, it calls for an inward act to match it . . . clarify, clarify.

October 6th

A DAY when I am expecting someone for lunch is quite unlike ordinary days. There is a reason to make the flowers look beautiful all over the house, and I know that Anne Woodson, who is coming today, will notice them, for she sees this house in a way that few of my friends do, perhaps because she has lived here without me, has lived her way into the place by pruning and weeding, and once even tidying the linen cupboard!

It is a mellow day, very gentle. The ash has lost its leaves and when I went out to get the mail and stopped to look up at it, I rejoiced to think that soon everything here will be honed down to structure. It is all a rich farewell now to leaves, to color. I think of the trees and how simply they let go, let fall the riches of a season, how without grief (it seems) they can let go and go deep into their roots for renewal and sleep. Eliot's statement comes back to me these days:

> Teach us to care and not to care
> Teach us to sit still.

It is there in Mahler's *Der Abschied*, which I play again every autumn (Bruno Walter with Kathleen Ferrier). But in Mahler it is a cry of loss, a long lyrical cry just *before* letting go, at least until those last long phrases that suggest peace, renunciation. But I think of it as the golden leaves and the brilliant small red maple that shone transparent against the shimmer of the lake yesterday when I went over to have a picnic with Helen Milbank.

Does anything in nature despair except man? An animal with a foot caught in a trap does not seem to despair. It is too busy trying to survive. It is all closed in, to a kind of still, intense waiting. Is this a key? Keep busy with survival. Imitate the trees. Learn to lose in order to recover, and remember that nothing stays the same for long, not even pain, psychic pain. Sit it out. Let it all pass. Let it go.

Yesterday I weeded out violets from the iris bed. The iris was being choked by thick bunches of roots, so much like fruit under the earth. I found one single very fragrant violet and some small autumn crocuses. Now, after an hour's work as the light failed and I drank in the damp smell of earth, it looks orderly again.

October 8th

I DON'T know whether the inward work is achieving something or whether it is simply the autumn light, but I begin to see my way again, which means to resume *myself*. This morning two small miracles took place. When, still in bed, I looked out of my window (it is a soft misty morning), it happened that "light was on half the rock" out in the meadow. I understand now why that line of Gogarty's has haunted me for years, for when I saw light on half that granite boulder, I felt a stab of pure joy. Later on when I was wandering around watering flowers, I was stopped at the threshold of my study by a ray on a Korean chrysanthemum, lighting it up like a spotlight, deep red petals and Chinese yellow center, glowing, while the lavender aster back of it was in shadow with a salmon-pink spray of peony leaves and the barberry Eleanor picked for me. Seeing it was like getting a transfusion of autumn light right to the vein.

Arnold came to begin work on a new barn floor. It is all rot under the big boards and going to be a more expensive job than we thought at first, but that is the way it always is.

Yesterday Anne and I had two beautiful excursions, the first to the Ledges where there are still fringed gentians in the field. That vivid blue standing up in the cut stubble is extravagantly exciting. I can never quite believe the gentians will be there and for a time we couldn't see one; but as we walked on, they began to appear, one by one, three or four flowers on a stem. Afterward we sat for a while by Silver Lake, perfectly still, a mirror with the mountain like a pale blue ghost at the end, light through the brilliant red rock maple. Perfect peace.

I never see Anne without learning something I didn't know. There are still monarch butterflies floating about. We looked long at one, the slow pulse, as it sucked sweetness from an autumn crocus here in the garden. Anne told me the monarchs are migrating now to Brazil. Is it Brazil? Anyway, thousands of miles to the south.

She brought two paintings—one an illustration of my sonnet "The Light Years," the other the conjunction of red shirley poppies greatly enlarged, with one of the ancient slate gravestones from our cemetery. Memento Mori in the midst of the most fragile of lives, the poppy's. Anne is using a flat technique and the danger, of course, is that the painting may end by being merely "decorative," without nuance. But this one seems to me successful. Anne's genius is in this kind of poetic synthesis, a vision of things as they are.

Once more poetry is for me the soul-making tool. Perhaps I am learning at last to let go, and that is what this resurgence of poetry is all about.

October 9th

HAS IT REALLY happened at last? I feel released from the rack, set free, in touch with the deep source that is only *good*, where poetry lives. We have waited long this year for the glory, but suddenly the big maple is all gold and the beeches yellow with a touch of green that makes the yellow even more intense. There are still nasturtiums to be picked, and now I must get seriously to work to get the remaining bulbs in.

It has been stupidly difficult to let go, but that is what has been needed. I had allowed myself to get overanxious, clutching at what seemed sure to pass, and clutching is the surest way to murder love, as if it were a kitten, not to be squeezed so hard, or a flower to fade in a tight hand. Letting go, I have come back yesterday and today to a sense of my life here in all its riches, depth, freedom for soul-making.

It's a real break-through. I have not written in sonnet form for a long time, but at every major crisis in my life when I reach a point of clarification, where pain is transcended by the quality of the experience itself, sonnets come. Whole lines run through my head and I cannot *stop* writing until whatever it is gets said.

Found three huge mushrooms when I went out before breakfast to fill the bird feeder. So far only jays come, but the word will get around.

October 11th

THE JOKE is on me. I filled this weekend with friends so that I would not go down into depression, not knowing that I should have turned the corner and be writing poems. It is the climactic moment of autumn, but already I feel like Sleeping Beauty as the carpet of leaves on the front lawn gets thicker and thicker. The avenue of beeches as I drive up the winding road along the brook is glorious beyond words, wall on wall of transparent gold. Laurie Armstrong came for roast beef Sunday dinner. Then I went out for two hours late in the afternoon and put in a hundred tulips. In itself that would not be a big job, but everywhere I have to clear space for them, weed, divide perennials, rescue iris that is being choked by violets. I really get to weeding only in spring and autumn, so I am working through a jungle now. Doing it I feel strenuously happy and at peace. At the end of the afternoon on a gray day, the light is sad and one feels the chill, but the bitter smell of earth is a tonic.

I can hardly believe that relief from the anguish of these past months is here to stay, but so far it does feel like a true change of mood—or rather, a change of *being* where I can stand alone. So much of my life here is precarious. I cannot always believe even in my work. But I have come in these last days to feel again the validity of my struggle here, that it is meaningful whether I ever "succeed" as a writer or not, and that even its failures, failures of nerve, failures due to a difficult temperament, can be meaningful. It is an age where more and more human beings are caught up in lives where fewer and fewer inward decisions can be made, where fewer and fewer real choices exist. The fact that a middle-aged, single woman, without any vestige of family left, lives in this house in a silent village and is responsible only to her own soul means something. The fact that she is a writer and can tell where she is and what it is like on the pilgrimage inward can be of comfort. It is comforting to know there are light-house keepers on rocky islands along the coast. Sometimes, when I have been for a walk after dark and see my house lighted up, looking so alive, I feel that my presence here is worth all the Hell.

I have time to think. That is the great, the greatest luxury. I have time to be. Therefore my responsibility is huge. To use time well and to be all that I can in whatever years are left to me. This does not dismay. The dismay comes when I lose the sense of my life as connected (as if by an aerial) to many, many other lives whom I do not even know and cannot ever know. The signals go out and come in all the time.

Why is it that poetry always seems to me so much more a true work of the soul than prose? I never feel elated after writing a page of prose, though I have written good things on concentrated will, and at least in a novel the imagination is fully engaged. Perhaps it is that prose is earned and poetry given. Both can be revised almost indefinitely. I do not mean to say that I do not work at poetry. When I am really inspired I can put a poem through a hundred drafts and keep my excitement. But this sustained battle is possible only when I am in a state of grace, when the deep channels are open, and when they are, when I am both profoundly stirred and balanced, then poetry comes as a gift from powers beyond my will.

I have often imagined that if I were in solitary confinement for an indefinite time and knew that no one would ever read what I wrote, I would still write poetry, but I would not write novels. Why? Perhaps because the poem is primarily a dialogue with the self and the novel a dialogue with others. They come from entirely different modes of being. I suppose I have written novels to find out what I *thought* about something and poems to find out what I *felt* about something.

Photo by Eleanor Blair

October 14th

TROPICAL AND DEPLETING weather again. The leaves from the big maples are nearly gone, but below the garden there is still a glowing golden screen of beeches. And all around the house such a thick carpet of leaves I feel half buried. The Warners are here now raking, thank goodness—it feels like a rescue.

Gray sky. No lift. There is a danger with the sonnets that I may write too much, too fast, carried along on the flood instead of controling and shaping it. A sign of fatigue.

Yesterday I had a wonderful day with Danny, a man of twenty who has grown a lot of wisdom through suffering. We recognize each other as fellow sufferers, possibly sufferers for the same reason, an acute awareness beyond what we are able to put into action or to *be*, as it were. He is going to become a great teacher.

I shall keep the image of him sitting against the window with golden leaves behind him, and his long reddish hair and fine head making him look more than ever like a Renaissance young man. He has become more solid these last years. The tremor is still there, but there is more muscle in him. We talked at length about loyalty, a subject much in my mind because I am often accused of disloyalty when I analyze my feelings. I expect it is a professional deformation, that of the novelist. More about this later. I have to think it out.

October 17th

THE LONG WARM AUTUMN has come to an end—hard frost last night, a cold gray sky. When I woke it was snowing! These are only flurries, but what a change! I picked the last nasturtiums yesterday. They are shriveled now, and even the parsley has been "touched." I have the very last bunch of garden flowers on my desk—a few yellow marigolds, one pale yellow and pink rose, and two others in bud. Now it will have to be florists' flowers with their awful sameness, none of the delightful home-grown mixtures of the spring, summer, and fall.

It has been next to impossible to keep at this journal lately because I am writing poems and they take the marrow of my energy. Things stir and buzz in my mind but do not get sorted out on paper. Today I want to think a little about loyalty, and it is a fact that I can think something out only by writing it. It is interesting that there is very little about loyalty under that heading in the *Oxford Book of Quotations* or in Bartlett; yet it must be one of the crucial concepts having to do with human relations, closely connected with trust. I am accused of disloyalty because I talk about things that many people would keep to themselves, and especially because I may discuss with people who "should not know" a human situation in which I am involved. I am not at all discreet about anything that concerns feeling. My business is the analysis of feeling.

It is the same with money—both human problems and money flow out of this house very freely, and I believe that is good. At least, it has to do in both cases with a vision of life, with an ethos. Might there be a valid distinction to be made between gossip (re human affairs) and boasting (re money) and this free flow in which I believe? I am always so astonished, after all the years when I had none, that I now have money to give away that sometimes I may speak of it out of sheer joy. No one who has inherited a fortune would ever do this, I suspect—*noblesse oblige.* No doubt it is shocking to some people. But I am really rather like a child who runs about saying, "Look at this treasure I found! I am going to give it to Peter, who is sad, or to Betty, who is sick." It reminds me of the old days with Kot* and James Stephens when we made up endless fantasies about what we would do when we were rich . . . and being *very* rich then meant not having to worry about every week's expenses! Being very rich so far as I am concerned is having a margin. The margin is being able to give.

I do not feel disloyal when I talk about my own life or that of the many others who pour in here in one way or another. What I am loyal to, I hope, is something more complex, i.e., I would not *use* things I know about anyone's private life to further my own ends. That would be both indiscreet and disloyal. But I believe we learn through the experiences of others as well as through our own, constantly meditating upon them, drawing the sustenance of human truth from them, and it seems natural to me to wish to share these *aperçus*, these questions, these oddities, these dilemmas and pangs. Why? Partly, I suppose, because the more one is a receptacle of human destinies, as I have become through

* S. S. Koteliansky.

my readers, the more one realizes how very few people could be called happy, how complex and demanding every deep human relationship is, how much real pain, anger, and despair are concealed by most people. And this is because many feel their own suffering is unique. It is comforting to know that we are all in the same boat. Into this house comes the despair now of many middle-aged women, to take one example.

I myself am engaged in trying to maintain a not altogether simple or easy human relationship in love that I talk about with true friends, for illumination. It has been immensely comforting lately to talk with D and to share what we are each learning through pain about our loves. I feel honored that we can talk as we do, and I do not feel it disloyal to the partners in each case. Why? Because it is "pure." We are sharing our experience in order better to understand it. D and I surely recognized each other the first time we talked some months ago. I have not felt this intimacy based on instant "recognition" so strongly since I first knew Bill Brown, thirty or more years ago. D and I are the same breed of cat, responsive and sensitive close to the surface, willing to give ourselves away. Such people rarely lead happy lives, but they do lead lives of constant growth and change. Gerald Heard's saying "he must go unprotected that he may be constantly changed" always comes to mind when I am speaking of what it is to be a poet and to go on writing poetry beyond the meridian of life. It is costly, so one has to hug very hard those like Bill Brown and D whom one has recognized.

October 28th

I woke this morning to a silver world, the meadow under a thick blanket of frost. The spruce boughs I laid on the flower beds yesterday afternoon looked as if someone had sprayed them silver . . . and a blue sky, and such light! I am working on a speech for Shreveport (go off next week to Dallas and Shreveport) on "The Delights of the Poet." The first delight I thought of was *light*. In this house the light has always been a presence—right now in a brilliant blue-green band on the sofa in the cozy room. A half hour ago it spotlit a pot of yellow chrysanthemums in there. I look out at trees leafless now except for one maple, where high up against the blue there is still branch after branch of translucent warm gold. The leaves sift down one by one like notes in music. This is the light we have been deprived of this queer autumn of tropical rains and gray skies, and it is good to have a taste of it.

Had a grand hour outdoors yesterday doing final jobs in the garden. An order of tulips and other bulbs still has not come, I presume because of the United Parcel strike, but I decided I had better cover the beds anyway in case we have an early snow. Win French brought four bales of hay and I undid them and laid thick pads along the sills of the north and east where the winter winds creep under the house. The Warners brought a pile of spruce and pine, and I was able to

cover all but three borders. It looked trim when I finished as
the dusk flooded in. The hills had been a warm rose, then
turned to purple, and just before the sun set it lit up the long
church windows bright flame.

The delights of the poet as I jotted them down turned
out to be light, solitude, the natural world, love, time, creation itself. Suddenly after the months of depression I am
fully alive in all these areas, and awake.

October 30th

LAST EVENING, after another of these perfectly radiant days, I
finished covering the garden. The second batch of branches
Bud Warner brought was almost all hemlock, much lighter
than the spruce and kinder to the spring shoots in April. As I
worked I came upon a deep purple viola in flower and two
autumn crocuses. They are on my desk in a small bisque Japanese jar. The crocuses opened at once to show delicate
purple veins on the lavender petals and the bright orange
stamens. The whole thing is such a wonder—the transparency of the crocus and the rich opaque viola petals and dark
green leaves—that I long to paint it, if only I could.

But the transcendent joy is the light now, the great
autumn light at last. There is nothing like this light anywhere else in the world so far as I know—the great glory of
New England. I have come back to my solitude, my joy, and
I am sure these radiant skies have much to do with it. That

little edge of ice in the air, too, is exhilarating. But I feel tired. Before a lecture trip I always go way down. When the time comes, I don't want to uproot, however much I may complain about the loneliness here.

With the return of cheerfulness I feel a sense of loss. The poems no longer flow out. I am more "normal" again, no longer that fountain of tears and intense feeling that I have been for months. Balance is achieved, or nearly. But at what price? Now I must write letters and try to clear the desk before I go. I have worked all week on a sonnet—hundreds of drafts—but it will *not* come out. Perhaps I have overworked it and killed it.

November 9th

HOME AGAIN to more radiant skies, a moon so bright last night I couldn't sleep. I found a huge box of bulbs; they have come at last. It is the eleventh hour as the ground will soon be frozen, but apparently a dock strike in Holland held them up.

The lectures went well. Both audiences, in Dallas and in Shreveport, listened intently; so at least once I experienced that marvelous stillness when I know a poem has really landed and is being heard as it can be only before a large impersonal group, because then I can "give tongue" and make whatever meaning and music is there "happen." Reading to one person, an intimate, I can never really let the

poem out. I found the going hard at first because I felt
dépaysé; after a long flight one is slightly out of balance, not
really settled in, still living one's way into the new atmosphere. And because, of course, it was in Texas more than ten
years ago, on a lecture trip, that I was wakened at seven
thirty A.M. with a long-distance call from Judy to say that my
father had died of a heart attack in a few minutes, after turning back in the taxi that was taking him to the airport to give
a lecture in Montreal. That memory and also the shadow of
the Kennedy assassination were much in my thoughts.

The psychological discomfort was acute at times. The
women I met were kind, and apparently gentle and responsive. Then suddenly that steely look comes into their eyes,
the real hatred of the Kennedys, *still*, after all the tragedies.
And besides that, of course, the closed door in the mind
when it comes to the race question. I know that it is there
partly as a symptom of loss, the loss of a loving warmth
between master and servant, the bewildering emergence of
Black Power that seems to these people a betrayal of old loy-
alties and old graces. But how well one comes to understand
in this atmosphere why many blacks have decided that all-
out war is the only way to change anything. Most of this I
had expected, but what upset me most was the selfishness;
the perimeter was so personal and limited. Does nothing, no
suffering outside it, ever break through, no need? The Kennedy assassination apparently has only closed the ring.

I felt culture in its deepest sense, what civilizes people, as
only a thin veneer, like the new houses which turn out to
have a brick façade pasted onto some other material. And
how incredible it was, in autumn, to swing past acres and
acres of fancy French provincial, Spanish, or Tudor houses
where not a leaf is allowed to rest on the immaculate lawns!

So beautiful in a *House and Garden* sort of way, so empty of poetry. For poetry lives in places where people work in their gardens or let them go wild and do not leave it to impersonal firms of gardeners to plant and trim.

Shreveport has far more charm, a livable town, where Dallas seems just plain inhuman, too rich, too new. A fifty-year-old building in Dallas looks antediluvian and "must be torn down." I felt the women were starved, starved for a kind of reality that does not exist in Neiman Marcus fur coats, in changes of fashion, in redecorating, in travel to the "right places." Under the polite small talk, one sensed nostalgia, the nostalgia of the bored child who does not know what he lacks, but knows he is being deprived of something essential to his well-being. These women are not disturbed, striving, anguished about the state of the world, not always guilty because they should be doing more as their equivalents in the East often are; also, they are not happy or fulfilled. It is hard to define, but under that huge sky and among so many "beautiful" things, houses, expensive cars, what I sensed was loneliness. There is too much luxury, maybe, and too little quality. Good manners are just not enough.

In the lectures I avoided politics and read no controversial poems, but at the lunches and in meeting people off the platform I said what I thought, and passionately, especially in the presence of someone gloating about a Kennedy child picked up for smoking pot!

I have an advantage in not having been born a damn Yankee, cannot be placed, in regional terms, beyond the pale, and so sometimes can say my say without giving offense.

But, oh, how marvelous it was to come home to dear shabby Cambridge, to uneven brick sidewalks, to untrimmed

gardens, to lawns covered with leaves, to young people walking hand in hand in absurd clothing, to dear Judy and the
pussies! We are all a little old and worn, but we are happy.
And Nelson, when I drove up under a pale bright sky, looked
like Heaven. I saw it freshly, saw the beauty of wooden clap-
board painted white, of old brick, of my own battered and
dying maples, as a shining marvel, a treasure that lifts the
mind and the heart and brings everyone who sees it back to
what *quality* is.

November 10th

I GOT the lily bulbs and the last of the tulips in yesterday
after a day of high pure skies, the hills turning purple just as
I finished. Today is bleak, a closed low cover of sky, no color.
It looks like rain or snow.

A bad day yesterday. I felt at sixes and sevens as though
I had not really landed, wrote too many letters, yet never
settled down, partly because Mohawk goes on strike
Wednesday night and I was to have left for New York
Thursday morning from Keene. This whole month is bits and
pieces of time with every weekend absorbed in one way or
another. Poetry has gone. No lines jump into my mind; the
taut thread gone slack.

I myself am slack. What is needed is a frame, an order, to
be once again established against the powerful current of letters to answer and the excitement of *Kinds of Love* coming

out. I am in a limbo that needs to be patterned from within. People who have regular jobs can have no idea of just this problem of ordering a day that has no pattern imposed on it from without. The light goes early. By four thirty in the afternoon I need electric light indoors, and, since gardening is over, that means inventing some regular chore such as (horrible thought!) getting the file room into order. In the mornings steady work at this journal, then copying and revising at least one poem for the book I plan for the spring of seventy-two to celebrate my sixtieth birthday. If there is motivation here, it is always self-ordering, self-exploratory, a perpetual keeping gear in order for that never-ending journey.

Another image I have of life here is that of a clearing-house. When too many messages pour in all at once the computer breaks down. Yesterday afternoon Z phoned twice, in a rather hysterical state. It reminded me of me at my worst—the jangled, weeping, self-justifying, miserable self of the bad days. Z is having a hard year, a year of personal loss and joblessness; at the same time she is trying to write a difficult novel (concerned with race relations, about which she knows a great deal).

For some unknown reason we got into a wrangle about—of all things!—best sellers. All aspiring writers say these things: "I will not compromise and write a best seller!"—as if they could! There may be a few totally faked-up books that sell, but on the whole I believe every writer writes as well as he can. It takes a good storyteller to write a best seller, and a good craftsman. The professional will never brush the best seller aside as something he could do if he were willing to compromise. No, it is all a matter of kinds of perception, and of kinds of writing. Very great writers—Dickens, Joyce, Trollope, Hemingway—have been best sellers. And very

great writers—Virginia Woolf, for example—have not, or only
by chance. (*The Years* was a best seller, but it is not her best
book.) We do the best we can and hope for the best, knowing that "the best," so far as selling goes, is a matter of chance.
The only thing that is not chance is what one asks of oneself
and how well or how badly one meets one's own standard.

I began the day with Vaughan Williams' *Mass* sung by
the King's College choir. There are days when only religious
music will do. Under the light of eternity things, the daily
trivia, the daily frustrations, fall away. It is all a matter of
getting to the center of the beam.

November 11th

LAST NIGHT I lay awake for a long time, a really good "think"
for a change. Perhaps it all began with my hearing of De
Gaulle's death and the chain of thoughts that followed on an
excellent short comment I heard on the car radio. The gist
was that the world mourns a whole man, and that whole men
are so rare that De Gaulle's loss is not only a loss to France
but to the world. The commentator also suggested that De
Gaulle had been most criticized for excessive patriotism, for
his mystique of France, by the very people who, had he been
of their own nation, would have praised him for the same
reason. The fact is that he did the impossible, and it is right
that he should be named with Roosevelt, Churchill, and
(alas) Stalin, for each has symbolized a nation's will to exist,

and the sense that its true self is most evident in times of crisis, and even of defeat. As I thought it all over, it seemed most remarkable that De Gaulle was able to preside over the end of the Algerian War and to bring it to a close in mutual regard, and without civil war at home—a triumph of integrity and moral fervor.

Wholeness, so far as statesmen go, may have something to do with speaking in one's own words. De Gaulle did not call in "writers"; the very idea is grotesque. The leader who allows others to speak for him is abdicating. Who is speaking via Nixon? Who wrote this phrase or that? One is never quite sure. He and Agnew become puppets. Who is the ventriloquist who manipulates them? The silent majority, the consensus, the imaginary public who will deliver the votes? One has only to place this atmosphere against that of De Gaulle, even the De Gaulle accused of behaving like a king rather than an elected representative of the people, to perceive the difference.

So, at the end of my think, it was not the word "grandeur" or "greatness" that stayed with me, but "wholeness." It occurs to me that this is often a masculine attribute (my father had it, not my mother) and that perhaps it goes not only with dedication to noble ends, but with a certain simple-mindedness—the people who hew to the heart of the matter, who get hold of the big ideas. As Whitehead says, "Nobody can be a good reasoner unless by constant practice he has realized the importance of getting hold of the big ideas and hanging onto them like grim death."

We are whole or have intimations of what it means to be whole when the entire being—spirit, mind, nerves, flesh, the body itself—are concentrated toward a single end. I feel it when I am writing a poem. Churchill embodied it during the

Blitz. De Gaulle, perhaps more than any other leader of our time, was its exemplar. Wholeness does not, of course, necessarily mean being right in a deduction or an action. It does mean not being divided in spirit by conscience, by doubt, by fear. The Japanese call it being "one-pointed."

It may also go with limited sensibility or a sensibility limited in some areas. When I said above that women were rarely as whole as men, I felt I must go back and think some more. It is harder for women, perhaps, to be "one-pointed," much harder for them to clear space around whatever it is they want to do beyond household chores and family life. Their lives are fragmented . . . this is the cry I get in so many letters—the cry not so much for "a room of one's own" as time of one's own. Conflict becomes acute, whatever it may be about, when there is no margin left on any day in which to try at least to resolve it.

My father was theoretically a feminist, but when it came down to the nitty gritty of life he expected everything to be done for him, of course, by his wife. It was taken for granted that "his work" must come before anything else. He was both a European bourgeois in upbringing and a man of the nineteenth century, so my mother didn't have a prayer. My father didn't like her to work and never gave her credit for it, even in some years when she was designing embroidered dresses for Belgart in Washington, D.C., and made more money than he did. Her conflict—and it was acute—came from her deep belief in what he wanted to do and at the same time resentment of his attitude toward her and his total lack of understanding of what he asked of her. They simply could not discuss such matters. Here we have surely made enormous strides in my lifetime. Few young women today would not at least make a try at "having it out" before marrying. Women are at last becoming persons first and wives second, and that is as it should be.

Later on in the night I reached a quite different level of being. I was thinking about solitude, its supreme value. Here in Nelson I have been close to suicide more than once, and more than once have been close to a mystical experience of unity with the universe. The two states resemble each other: one has no wall, one is absolutely naked and diminished to essence. Then death would be the rejection of life because we cannot let go what we wish so hard to keep, but have to let go if we are to continue to grow.

When I talk about solitude I am really talking also about making space for that intense, hungry face at the window, starved cat, starved person. It is making space to *be there*. Lately a small tabby cat has comé every day and stared at me with a strange, intense look. Of course I put food out, night and morning. She is so terrified that she runs away at once when I open the door, but she comes back to eat ravenously as soon as I disappear. Yet her hunger is clearly not only for food. I long to take her in my arms and hear her purr with relief at finding shelter. Will she ever become tame enough for that, to give in to what she longs to have? It is such an intense look with which she scans my face at the door before she runs away. It is not a pleading look, simply a huge question: "Can I trust?" Our two gazes hang on its taut thread. I find it painful.

For a long time, for years, I have carried in my mind the excruciating image of plants, bulbs, in a cellar, trying to grow without light, putting out *white* shoots that will inevitably wither. It is time I examined this image. Until now it has simply made me wince and turn away, bury it, as really too terrible to contemplate.

Today, Armistice Day, there is no mail. It makes a huge emptiness around me, and I am going to try to use it well, to write a poem. I came home yesterday with Teilhard de Chardin's *The Divine Milieu*. I feel real hunger for meat of this kind, to get above the present personal problems I chew and chew to some larger air (a mixed metaphor, never mind). And now to work. May God be with me.

There is really only one possible prayer: Give me to do everything I do in the day with a sense of the sacredness of life. Give me to be in Your presence, God, even though I know it only as absence.

Tomorrow the world crashes in again. I go to New York.

November 16th

FOUR DAYS in New York of sumptuous living on every plane, including, I must say, hours of something like technological panic, the sheer horror of getting about this city which is close to unlivable. It rained and rained and rained. That meant no taxis. Buses are more human, but it was traumatic when Marion Hamilton and I tried to get down to First Avenue and Eighth Street from our hotel to the theatre. We went from bus to bus, up and down and across, and finally walked blocks and blocks over from Fifth Avenue. There are no restaurants near The Orpheum, so we finally landed in a joint for a sandwich and a drink.

Even getting into the city had been next to impossible for

me as Mohawk was on strike, and I finally had had to change planes in Boston. Travel has become more and more difficult. I armed myself in patience and before I finally got back here, I needed it. What used to be a gentle passage by train, that beautiful ride from Boston along the shore line, a good diner, a peaceful think-time, has become a matter of waiting and enduring, of carrying bags long distances, of cross taxi drivers, of battling to get a means of conveyance over the shortest distance. One arrives through the uproar of one's anxiety and panic, exhausted at the start.

November 17th

I DID SPEND some hours in airports completely absorbed by Robert Coles's second piece on Erik Erikson (*New Yorker*, November 14th), rich in that kind of insight that opens up new understanding of oneself and of what is happening *now*. I underlined this passage, Erikson speaking (in *Young Man Luther*): "Millions of boys face these problems and solve them in some way or another—they live, as Captain Ahab says, with half of their heart and only one of their lungs, and the world is the worst for it. Now and again, however, an individual is called upon (called by *whom*, only the theologians claim to know, and by *what*, only bad psychologists) to lift his individual patienthood to the level of a universal one and to try to solve for all what he could not solve for himself alone." The key word for me, of course, is "patienthood," for this is exactly what is involved for the poet or artist of either sex. Coles himself says elsewhere in the piece, "Not everyone can or will do that—give his specific fears and desires a chance to be of universal significance." To do this takes a curious combination of humility, excruciating honesty, *and* (there's the rub) a sense of destiny or of identity. One must believe that private dilemmas are, if deeply examined, universal, and so, if expressed, have a human value beyond the private, and one must also believe in the vehicle for expressing them, in the talent.

In New York I saw publishers and Diarmuid, my agent. As always in the market place, all that happens to a work of art when it becomes public fills me with woe and anxiety. My novel will be out next week; I learned that success will depend on whether booksellers reorder within the first week! *Les jeux sont faits.* I have only to wait, but it is nerve-wracking.

Marion and I went to see the O'Keeffe retrospective at the Whitney, then down a flight to Eakins, also a huge show. It is interesting to observe that what O'Keeffe wanted to achieve was achieved from the start, and has hardly changed —the reducing of a landscape, a flower, or whatever to essence, the isolation of a powerful image which she then enlarges. Sometimes the effect is merely pictorial, and becomes banal and even sentimental (the famous skull with roses), but at her best a very few lines and blocks of color carry an explosive and mystical power. These are paintings that expand the mind, and I imagine living with one very happily.

The contrast with Eakins and all the questions it raised was absorbing, but unfortunately I was tired by then, too tired to see the latter with primary intensity. Where O'Keeffe is detached, abstract, rarely dealing with human beings, Eakins pores over the human face, and at his best gives us portraits that probe the whole person, and act upon the viewer as if an entire novel had been encapsulated there. I think of the ultrasensitive face of a maiden lady (who might have been Jane Tuttle in my novel), of certain men absorbed in thought. What other painter has so managed to catch a thinking face, except Rembrandt? Then there are the equally moving paintings of boys swimming, and here also the flesh is rendered not so much as light and shadow, as texture, but as terribly human and fragile—it is painterly but in a very unfashionable way, subtle and tender. How little nuance there seems to be any more!

We went to see *The Me Nobody Knows*, a rock-and-roll musical, the libretto put together from a book of poems written by ghetto children and sung and acted by a score of black, white, and Puerto Rican kids, none over eighteen. The impact was tremendous. I have rarely been so seized and shaken in the theatre. Freshness, attack, poetry, anger—a liberating evening full of tears of joy and rage. When such things are possible in the theatre, there is still hope.

Nothing could have been stranger than to follow *The Me Nobody Knows* with a matinée, the next afternoon, of the English play *Home*, acted magnificently by Ralph Richardson and John Gielgud as two old men who, one gradually comes to understand, are in a mental institution. They try to communicate, in half sentences, in asides, in silence . . . tentative, excruciatingly painful. There is no catharsis, and I found the tension nearly unbearable. Unforgettable, Gielgud staring out at the sky (facing the audience), watching imaginary clouds, and then every now and then tears streaming slowly down his cheeks. This too is everyman, just as the children were, shouting their last song, "Let me come in!" at the audience.

The big question, I jotted down during the long wait at the airport, is how to hope and what to hope *for*. We are citizens of a corrupt country, of a corrupt vision. There is such a sense of death and of being buried under the weight of technocracy. How to keep cool and get hold of the essential ... and, above all, how to recognize the essential. During *The Me Nobody Knows* we were in the very potent presence of it. It is going back to childhood—its riches, its terrible deprivations—that brings it home. There is the source.

After the incessant noise, shattering screams in the night, whining nerve-wracking garbage trucks, relentless pounding of road-breaking machinery, grinding of brakes, sirens, trucks roaring down Second Avenue, the silence of Nelson and today the marvelous white light of November came back to me with the impact of revelation.

November 18th

CARS GO BY, one by one, toward the village green, for the Ladies' Aid Sale takes place today in the old brick schoolhouse. A perfect day ... diffused clouds high in the air make the light rather tender. Sunlight on the white lintel of the door into the cozy room and then making a brilliant band on the blue-green couch in there.

I woke happy, anxious to get to the desk, to think and

maybe work at a poem, for I am eager now to begin revising (for the new book) those poems written last year, too fast, at the end of a long morning at the novel. But, as so often happens, I got bogged down almost at once in obligations—to answer a letter from a child about *The Fur Person*, to answer ... But at that moment two sacks of birdseed arrived from the Farmers' Exchange. Now I use two sacks in two weeks, fifty pounds, but soon it will be two in one week, then more for the greedy jays and squirrels, as well as evening grosbeaks, chickadees, nuthatches. I then wrote a blurb for a friend's book that I finished reading last night, and answered a long letter from a Professor Carolyn Heilbrun who may do an article on my work. She had sent me several reprints; I dived into one on Bloomsbury at once.

What a relief to find an essay that neither sneers at nor disparages Virginia Woolf! The sheer vital energy of the Woolfs always astonishes me when I stop to consider what they accomplished on any given day. Fragile she may have been, living on the edge of psychic disturbance, but think what she managed to do nonetheless—not only the novels (every one a break-through in form), but all those essays and reviews, all the work of the Hogarth Press, not only reading mss. and editing, but, at least at the start, packing the books to go out! And, besides all that, they lived such an intense social life. (When I went there for tea, they were always going out for dinner and often to a party later on.) The gaiety and fun of it all, the huge sense of *life*! The long, long walks through London that Elizabeth Bowen told me about. And two houses to keep going! Who of us could have accomplished what she did?

There may be a lot of self-involvement in the *Writer's Journal*, but there is no self-pity (and one has to remember that what Leonard published at that time was only a small part of all the journals, the part that concerned her work, so it *had* to be self-involved). It is painful that such genius should evoke such mean-spirited response at present. Is genius so common that we can afford to brush it aside? What does it matter whether she is major or minor, whether she imitated Joyce (I believe she did not), whether her genius was a limited one, limited by class? What remains true is that one cannot pick up a single one of her books and read a page without feeling more alive. If art is not to be life-enhancing, what is it to be? Half the world is feminine—why is there resentment at a female-oriented art? Nobody asks *The Tale of Genji* to be masculine! Women certainly learn a lot from books oriented toward a masculine world. Why is not the reverse also true? Or are men really so afraid of women's creativity (because they are not themselves at the center of creation, cannot bear children) that a woman writer of genius evokes murderous rage, must be brushed aside with a sneer as "irrelevant"?

When I was young and knew Virginia Woolf slightly, I learned something that startled me—that a person may be ultrasensitive and not warm. She was intensely curious and plied one with questions, teasing, charming questions that made the young person glow at being even for a moment the object of her attention. But I did feel at times as though I were "a specimen American young poet" to be absorbed and filed away in the novelist's store of vicarious experience. Then one had also the daring sense that anything could be said, the sense of freedom that was surely one of the keys to the Bloomsbury ethos, a shared secret amusement at human folly or pretensions. She was immensely kind to have seen me for at least one tea, as she did for some years whenever I was in England, but in all that time I never felt warmth, and this was startling.

December 1st

THE DARKNESS AGAIN. An annihilating review in the Sunday *Times*. I must have had a premonition, as I felt terribly low in my mind all weekend. Now it is the old struggle to survive, the feeling that I have created twenty-four "children" and every one has been strangled by lack of serious critical attention. This review is simply stupid. But what hurts is the lack of respect shown by Francis Brown in not getting a reviewer who had some knowledge of my work and would be able to get inside it with sympathetic understanding. It is odd that nonfiction appears to get a better break these days than fiction. On a deeper level I have come to believe (perhaps that is one way to survive) that there is a reason for these repeated blows—that I am not meant for success and that in a way adversity is my climate. The inner person thrives on it. The challenge is there to go deeper.

What a lonely business it is ... from the long hours of uncertainty, anxiety, and terrible effort while writing such a long book, to the wild hopes (for it looked like a possible best seller, and the *Digest* has it for their condensed books) and the inevitable disaster at the end. I have had many good reviews and cannot really complain about that. What I have not had is the respect due what is now a considerable opus. I am way outside somewhere in the wilderness. And it has been a long time of being in the wilderness. But I would be crazy if I didn't believe that I deserve better, and that eventually it will come out right. The alternative is suicide and I'm not about to indulge in that fantasy of revenge.

Somehow the great clouds made the day all right, a gift of splendor as they sailed over our heads.

December 2nd

I OPENED Teilhard de Chardin (*The Divine Milieu*) to this passage this morning:

> The masters of the spiritual life incessantly repeat that God wants only souls. To give those words their true value, we must not forget that the human soul, however independently created our philosophy represents it as being, is inseparable, in its birth and in its growth, from the universe into which it is born. In each soul, God loves and partly saves the whole world which that soul sums up in an incommunicable and particular way. But this summing-up, this welding, are not given to us ready-made and complete with the first awakening of consciousness. It is we who, through our own activity, must industriously assemble the widely scattered elements. The labour of seaweed as it concentrates in its tissues the substances scattered, in infinitesimal quantities, throughout the vast layers of ocean; the industry of

bees as they make honey from the juices broadcast in so
many flowers—these are but pale images of the ceaseless
working-over that all the forces of the universe undergo
in us in order to reach the level of spirit.

Thus, every man, in the course of his life, must not
only show himself obedient and docile. By his fidelity
he must *build*—starting with the most natural territory
of his own self—a work, an *opus*, into which something
enters from all the elements of the earth. *He makes his
own soul* throughout his earthly days; and at the same
time he collaborates in another work, in another *opus*,
which infinitely transcends, while at the same time it
narrowly determines, the perspectives of his individual
achievement: the completing of the world.

It is only when we can believe that we are creating the
soul that life has any meaning, but when we can believe it—
and I do and always have—then there is nothing we do that
is without meaning and nothing that we suffer that does not
hold the seed of creation in it. I have become convinced
since that horrible review (unimportant in itself) that it is a
message, however deviously presented, to tell me that I have
been overconcerned with the materialistic aspects of bringing out this novel, the dangerous hope that it become a best
seller, or that, for once, I might get a leg up from the critics,
the establishment, and not have once more to see the work
itself stand alone and make its way, heart by heart, as it is
discovered by a few people with all the excitement of a
person who finds a wildflower in the woods that *he* has discovered on his own. From my isolation to the isolation of
someone somewhere who will find my work there exists a
true communion. I have not lacked it in these last years, and
it is a blessing. It is free of "ambition" and it "makes the

world go away," as the popular song says. This is what I can hope for and I must hope for nothing more or less.

Thinking of writers I cherish—Traherne, George Herbert, Simone Weil, and the novelists Turgenev, Trollope, Henry James, Virginia Woolf, E. M. Forster, all of them modest, private, "self-actualizers"—I see that they are all outside the main stream of what is expected *now*. The moderate human voice, what might be called "the human milieu"—this is supremely unfashionable and appears even to be irrelevant. But there always have been and always will be people who can breathe only there and who are starved for nourishment. I am one of those readers and I am also one who can occasionally provide this food. That is all that really matters to me this morning.

January 2nd

BEGIN AGAIN where this long hiatus of Christmas and the book's publication began just a month ago.

I can understand people simply fleeing the mountainous effort Christmas has become even for those, like me, without children. Everyone must feel revolt as I do about the middle of December when I am buried under the necessity of finding presents, the immense effort of wrapping and sending, and the never-ended guilt about unsent cards, about letters. But there are always a few saving graces and finally they make up for all the bother and distress.

One such moment came as I turned into Harrisville from

Dublin and saw what looked at first like a prehistoric animal coming toward me. Then I realized that it was a Christmas tree carried on a man's shoulder, pointed toward me. There he was, bringing home the tree through the silent, woodsy, white world. We had a huge snow, fifteen inches, December 16th. Luckily it had been announced and I managed to get Judy and the two cats up here a day early; so we enjoyed it in perfect peace, open fires burning, and the moony, whirling world outside as if we were in the center of a "snowing" glass paperweight.

Before that, since a lunch was cancelled because of the snow, I was suddenly given a few hours of unexpected time and managed to get down a poem that had been pursuing me for days.

What other saving graces in the welter of *things*? The dear presents made for me by friends, often far away, sometimes friends I have never seen who know me only through my work—a knitted waistcoat, a lovely soft white wool sweater, a strawberry-pink turtleneck. How cherished they make me feel! Eva Le Gallienne made me a superb long heavy wool scarf to wear when I go out to feed the birds. Anne Woodson designed and worked a small petit-point pillow, quoting the last lines of the Kali poem—a bold design of light and dark with two shirley poppies woven through it. I wept with the sheer joy of it, and the love it represents, when I opened it:

> Help us to be the always hopeful
> Gardeners of the spirit
> Who know that without darkness
> Nothing comes to birth
> As without light
> Nothing flowers. *

* *A Grain of Mustard Seed.*

This December I have been more aware than ever before of the meaning of a festival of light coming as it does when the days are so short, and we live in darkness for the greater part of the afternoon. Candlelight, tree lights—ours, tiny ones—are reflected in all the windows from four o'clock on.

Then there are the great presents of long letters from former students and friends from whom I hear only once a year. They bring me a tapestry of lives, a little overwhelming, but interesting in their conjunctions. Two of my best poets at Wellesley, two girls who had something like genius, each married and each stopped writing altogether. Now this year each is moving toward poetry again. That news made me happy. It also made me aware once more of how rarely a woman is able to continue to create after she marries and has children.

Whatever college does not do, it does create a climate where work is demanded and where nearly every student finds him- or herself meeting the demand with powers he did not know he had. Then quite suddenly a young woman, if she marries, has to diverge completely from this way of life, while her husband simply goes on toward the goals set in college. She is expected to cope not with ideas, but with cooking food, washing dishes, doing laundry, and if she insists on keeping at a job, she needs both a lot of energy and the ability to organize her time. If she has an infant to care for, the jump from the intellectual life to that of being a nurse must be immense. "The work" she may long to do has been replaced by various kinds of labor for which she has been totally unprepared. She has longed for children, let us say, she is deeply in love, she has what she thought she wanted, so she suffers guilt and dismay to feel so disoriented. Young husbands these days can and do help with the chores and, far more important, are aware of the problem and will talk anxiously about it—anxiously because a wife's conflict affects their peace of mind. But the fact remains that, in marrying, the wife has suffered an earthquake and the husband has not. His goals have not been radically changed; his mode of being has not been radically changed.

I shall copy out parts of one of these letters, as it gave me much to ponder on and I shall refer to it again in the weeks to come, no doubt. K says,

> It has been a year of unusual branching out, and I feel quite young. You will laugh at that, but many of our friends now are pathetically worried about aging and full of envy for young people and regrets about wasting their own youth—and these are parents of small children, under thirty! I think it is a very destructive system indeed that worships youth the way we Americans do and gives young people no ideals of maturity to reach for, nothing to look forward to. (Adolescence is often so miserable that one needs an incentive to get through it!)
>
> Well, I'd better stop, because I feel a harangue coming on; I'm so hopelessly out of tune with these times and it's a temptation to join the haranguers. . . .
>
> As for the writing of poems, I'm beginning to see that *the* obstruction is being female, a fact I have never accepted or known how to live with. I wish that I could talk to you about it; I know that you are into insights that I'm only beginning to realize *exist*. (And that's why Sylvia Plath interests me; Robert Lowell describes her as ' "feminine rather than female'," whatever that means; but she strikes me as breaking through the feminine to something natural that, while I suppose it still has a sex, can't be called feminine even.) At least I can

see the inadequacy of that male and very Freudian psychiatrist, trying to help me accept or do something with
this burden of femininity that marriage had seemed to
finalize. I am grateful to all the crazies out there in the
Women's Liberation; we *need* them as outrageous
mythical characters to make our hostilities and dilemmas really visible. As shallow as my contact with the
Women's Liberation has been, I have really seen something new about myself this year; the old stalemated
internal conflict has been thrown off balance and I am
surprised to understand how much of my savage hostility is against men. I have always been rejecting language because it *is* a male invention. My voice in my
own poems, though coming out of myself, became a
masculine voice on the page, and I felt the need to
destroy that voice, that role, in making room for D in
my life. It is not just my equation but a whole family
tradition, which decrees a deep and painful timidity for
the women; and for me this was always especially intol-
erable, since the personality I was born with was the
very opposite of passive! It is very fortunate for me
that, of all my friends, excepting you, D is the only one
who seems to understand, or at least to sympathize with
this—a fact which violates the principles of psychiatry
since he is the one most threatened by any sexual crisis
I may undergo, the target most at hand for hostilities
against men, and the most disturbed by the instability
that comes with my trying to readjust the balance of my
mind.

This letter goes to the heart of the matter. I found it
deeply disturbing. For what is really at stake is unbelief in
the woman as artist, as creator. K no longer sees her talent as
relevant or valid, language itself as a masculine invention.
That certainly closes the door with a bang! But I believe it

will open because the thrust of a talent as real as hers must finally break through an intellectual formula and assert what she now denies. What she writes eventually will be in her own voice. Every now and then I meet a person whose speaking voice appears to be placed artificially, to come not from the center of the person, but from an unnatural register. I am thinking especially of women with high, strained voices. I know nothing about voice placement in a technical sense, but I have longed to say, "For God's sake, get down to earth and speak in your own voice!" This is not so much a matter of honesty, perhaps (K is excruciatingly honest), as of self-assurance: I am who I am.

January 5th

AND NOW it is time that I laid aside, at least for a few hours a day, the world that pours in here from the outside, and resumed my own life in this nunnery where one woman meditates alone. But there is no way of "laying aside" a knock at the door. Yesterday afternoon, after hours of answering letters in quiet desperation, I decided to wash the bathroom floor and had just finished, dirty and triumphant, when the doorbell jangled and there outside in the sleeting snow was a woman from Ohio, on her way to Concord, who had simply decided to knock as she passed through Nelson. She had written me a week or so ago a long, good letter about *Kinds of Love*, one I had not yet answered, but luckily I did remember it. What people never realize is that I cannot remember every letter that falls in here, because there are so many from strangers, and I have to read them and then literally put them away from me to be able to breathe. She stayed half an hour and by doing so broke the slow rhythm of late afternoon, when I wander about doing odd jobs, answering a few cards, whatever comes easily and naturally, but do not ask myself to summon real psychic energy or deep response.

After that interruption the furnace suddenly went off; so I built a big fire in the cozy room to keep Punch, the parrot, warm, then called for help. The men were here in an hour. I shall never get used to this joy of living in the country—when help is needed, it is there.

At nine I forced myself to look at and listen to Nixon's nonconversation with four TV pundits. His answer that one cannot be asked to project a vibrant dream when in the middle of a nightmare summed it all up—his total lack of vision in the humane sense. For it is surely just in the nightmare time that vibrant dreams are born and can be communicated effectively ... Churchill in 1940, Roosevelt in the Depression years. What a cramped little soul comes through from Nixon! What was fascinating was the conjunction of this strangely dead hour with what followed immediately— an interview by Brinkley with six editors of high-school magazines, two blacks, a Chinese, four middle-class whites. These kids were articulate, caring, thoughtful, and realistic. But what has Nixon said to give them hope? Still, their talk warmed the cold air and I went to bed feeling happy about the future and in the thought of what the eighteen-year-old vote may do to change the crass defeatist atmosphere.

And now ... and now ... toward the inner world. Yesterday from D, who is carrying a fearful load at the moment as he is both getting an M.A. in education and teaching full time in a public high school: "Just an excruciatingly short note, May, to wish for you the absolute calm and unfathomed strength needed to face a gruelling year, a single day. We see little of each other, but we fight together, and we do not fail." Among the best memories of 1970 are those two long conversations I had with D about our private lives, about love. We recognized each other as the same breed, those who must find a balance between going naked (in the Yeatsian sense, "There's more enterprise in walking naked") and being tough enough to survive such intensity of caring and such openness, between a driving need to share experience and the need for time to experience, and that means solitude, a balance between the need to become oneself and to give of oneself . . . and of course they are closely related. D is very aware of the problems of women, sensitive to the needs of a woman lover for her own independence, her own growth; he has suffered because he is generous. But he has also had the guts to cut off what did not and could not work. It was especially illuminating to me as I ponder the problems of women to see it, in this instance, from the other side. D has been expected to accept unfaithfulness without demur ("I have to have my independence"), an absolute demand not to be pinned down in any way, and what looks from where I sit like plain cruelty. He is younger than his girl by seven years or so, but very much older in wisdom. I have the greatest respect for this man. Would he be what he is in his early twenties if he had not gone through suicidal depression at thirteen or fourteen, followed by years of psychiatry? He has very great strength now, strength also to carry a big load of work. I think of him and of those much younger kids on

TV last night with such a surge of hope and faith, and with humility. At his age I was a good lover only in the romantic sense of the word—I had not even begun to think of the "other" as he does, and I was ambitious in a rather cheap way.

It is hope-giving to consider the young, and it is also hope-giving to consider growth as a constant. Here I am at fifty-eight and in this past year I have only begun to understand what loving is ... forced to my knees again and again like a gardener planting bulbs or weeding, so that I may once more bring a relationship to flower, keep it truly alive.

I am reading the letters of Carrington, the young woman painter who attached herself so fervently and selflessly to Lytton Strachey and committed suicide shortly after his death. The book is disturbing. There is something in me that resents so much talk about feeling and so many personal interchanges. Yet the strength of Bloomsbury may have been just this—their fantastic honesty about personal life. They accepted that in a given lifetime there are going to be many and complex relationships that nourish, and many kinds of love. They accepted that nearly everyone concerned with the arts is going to have to come to terms with sexual ambivalence, and to cope with being bisexual, and that passionate friendships may include sex. (How sane this appears after the revolting male exhibitionism and role-playing of Miller, Mailer, and Hemingway!) They achieved not only an amazing richness of production of works of art (in painting, poetry, the novel) that were seminal, works of economics that were also seminal, but led extraordinary lives without becoming messy or self-indulgent. If they were neurotics, and perhaps they were, they were civilized and civilizing neurotics. They are resented especially by Americans because within our puritanical ethos it doesn't seem quite "right." We can accept far more readily the confessed neurotic, drug-taking or whatever, who edifies by his horrible example! They were simply a little too good to be true. How hard they worked, and what fun they had! Maybe the gossip, incessant, witty, and sometimes malicious, occasionally offends our sense of decorum—with reason. But decorum seemed to them, no doubt, altogether a matter of *how* things are done, not *what* things are said or done.

Presumably Willa Cather lived a private life of some intensity, but she was exceedingly careful to keep it out of the public eye, even to the extent of forbidding the publication of any letter after her death. How very different this attitude to Virginia Woolf's open admission that *Orlando* was based on her friendship with Vita Sackville-West. Is it, here in America, parents who stand in the way? The fear of hurting a parent if one is honest?

My own belief is that one regards oneself, if one is a serious writer, as an instrument for experiencing. Life—all of it— flows through this instrument and is distilled through it into works of art. How one lives as a private person is intimately bound into the work. And at some point I believe one has to stop holding back for fear of alienating some imaginary reader or real relative or friend, and come out with personal truth. If we are to understand the human condition, and if we are to accept ourselves in all the complexity, self-doubt, extravagance of feeling, guilt, joy, the slow freeing of the self to its full capacity for action and creation, both as human being and as artist, we have to know all we can about each other, and we have to be willing to go naked.

Photo by Mort Mace

January 7th

I HAVE WORKED all morning—and it is now afternoon—to try to make by sheer art and craft an ending to the first stanza of a lyric that shot through my head intact. I should not feel so pressed for time, but I do, and I suppose I always shall. Yeats speaks of spending a week on one stanza. The danger, of course, is overmanipulation, when one finds oneself manipulating *words*, not images or concepts. My problem was to make a transition viable between lovers in a snowstorm and the whiteness of a huge amaryllis I look at across the hall in the cosy room—seven huge flowers that make constant silent hosannas as I sit here.

In a period of happy and fruitful isolation such as this, any interruption, any intrusion of the social, any obligation breaks the thread on my loom, breaks the pattern. Two nights ago I was called at the last minute to attend the caucus of Town Meeting ... and it threw me. But at least the companionship gave me one insight: a neighbor told me she had been in a small car accident and had managed to persuade the local paper to ignore her true age (as it appears on her license) and to print her age as thirty-nine! I was really astonished by this confidence. I am proud of being fifty-eight, and still alive and kicking, in love, more creative, balanced, and potent than I have ever been. I mind certain physical deteriorations, but not *really*. And not at all when I

look at the marvelous photograph that Bill sent me of Isak
Dinesen just before she died. For after all we make our faces
as we go along, and who when young could ever look as she
does? The ineffable sweetness of the smile, the total acceptance and joy one receives from it, life, death, everything
taken in and, as it were, savored—and let go.

Wrinkles here and there seem unimportant compared to
the *Gestalt* of the whole person I have become in this past
year. Somewhere in *The Poet and the Donkey* Andy speaks
for me when he says, "Do not deprive me of my age. I have
earned it."

My neighbor's wish to be known forever as thirty-nine
years old made me think again of what K said in her letter
about the people in their thirties mourning their lost youth
because we have given them no ethos that makes maturity
appear an asset. Yet we have many examples before us. It
looks as if T. S. Eliot came into a fully consummated happy
marriage only when he was seventy. Yeats married when he
was fifty or over. I am coming into the most fulfilled love of
my life now. But for some reason Americans are terrified of
the very idea of passionate love going on past middle age.
Are they afraid of being alive? Do they want to be dead, i.e.,
safe? For of course one is never safe when in love. Growth is
demanding and may seem dangerous, for there is loss as well
as gain in growth. But why go on living if one has ceased to
grow? And what more demanding atmosphere for growth
than love in any form, than any relationship which can call
out and requires of us our most secret and deepest selves?

My neighbor who wishes to remain thirty-nine indefinitely does so out of anxiety—she is afraid she will no longer
be "attractive" if people know her age. But if one wants
mature relationships, one will look for them among one's

peers. I cannot imagine being in love with someone much younger than I because I have looked on love as an *éducation sentimentale*. About love I have little to learn from the young.

January 8th

YESTERDAY was a strange, hurried, uncentered day; yet I did not have to go out, the sun shone. Today I feel centered and time is a friend instead of the old enemy. It was zero this morning. I have a fire burning in my study, yellow roses and mimosa on my desk. There is an atmosphere of festival, of release, in the house. We are one, the house and I, and I am happy to be alone—time to think, time to be. This kind of open-ended time is the only luxury that really counts and I feel stupendously rich to have it. And for the moment I have a sense of fulfillment both about my life and about my work that I have rarely experienced until this year, or perhaps until these last weeks. I look to my left and the transparent blue sky behind a flame-colored cyclamen, lifting about thirty winged flowers to the light, makes an impression of stained glass, light-flooded. I have put the vast heap of unanswered letters into a box at my feet, so I don't see them. And now I am going to make one more try to get that poem right. The last line is still the problem.

January 12th

SNOWING TODAY. One should never assert that one feels well; something awful is sure to happen. The furies came to the window again two nights ago, and I had a frightful attack of temper, of nerves, of resentment against X, followed by the usual boomerang of acute anxiety. It is frightening to have regressed in this way, for I have not had an outburst like this for *months*. So much for whatever hubris I may have indulged in about driving the furies away for good. They know better.

No doubt any intimate relationship suffers this kind of stress now and then. The world inside explodes, often about a trivial thing, and resentment (always there in some measure) flares out. Afterward both people feel bruised, ashamed, survivors, but barely, of the unpremeditated ghastly attack upon each other. But perhaps the worst danger is to exaggerate its importance, and to allow oneself the panic I went into last night. I was in such anxiety that my hair was soaked through. The only other time I have experienced this was during an attack of acute physical pain, when I had diverticulitis and was in a hospital for a week.

At such times the whole being, physical and psychic, is literally unstrung, in an uproar, and we have to wait for the uproar to die down to know what has happened. I feel better this morning because X did call last night. We shall get back slowly to where we were before this seizure. One pays a high price, but like drunkards who swear with every hang-over, "never again!" the war against the unregenerate self goes on. The price is exhaustion of spirit. It was all I could do to get up, make the bed, wash the breakfast things. Nothing has any meaning for a time. My only source of comfort is that at least I did not go back to cigarettes. This is my fifth day without smoking. I still feel deprived of every "small pleasure," dull, and depressed. But I am determined, for X's sake as well as for my own, to share in the attempt to kick the habit.

This was interrupted by a wire from J to tell me that the sister with whom she has lived for many years died suddenly last night. What if it had happened to X while we were in a state of anger? One has only to set a loved human being against the fact that we are all in peril all the time to get back a sense of proportion. What does anything matter compared to the reality of love and its span, so brief at best, maintained against such odds?

I had intended to devote a day's journal to what I call "the usual" days here . . . and then the furies came to the window. Those days, apparently empty, are the most creative and most precious within their inexorable structure. When I am homesick for Nelson, as I was in Japan, I think of the usual days as Heaven. But just as a prisoner does (and in winter my life is imprisoned much of the time), I know it is essential for me to move within a structure. The bed must be made (it is what I hate doing most), the dishes washed, the place tidied up before I can go to work with a free mind. There must be rewards for hard tasks, and often a cigarette had been the reward for putting out rubbish or cleaning Punch's cage. In the winter, when I can't garden, I make an

effort to get at the chaos behind closed doors. This week I
have been cleaning out the glory hole upstairs—an incredible
welter of stuff from old snow boots to Christmas-tree orna-
ments, torn sheets, as well as the paraphernalia of a potting
shed. Win French is going to build me a long bench to lie
under the eave with four compartments for storage: winter
boots, blankets, winter clothes, and Christmas-tree orna-
ments. I have been here twelve years and it does seem amazing that I am only getting at this problem now. The truth is
that I moved in and immediately began to write and garden.
That was what I was after—a daily rhythm, a kind of fugue
of poetry, gardening, sleeping and waking in the house.
Nothing else mattered enough to take the time. I could
spend the whole day housekeeping, but I won't, as long as
total chaos is kept at bay and what my eyes rest on is beauty
and order. Only now and then the appalling state of a cupboard disturbs my mind enough so that it is worth tidying—
and then I must say it is a great satisfaction to get it done. In
the general routine of the year January is clean-up time and
seed-catalogue time. Ordering seeds is my reward for finish-
ing the income-tax figures.

I have been thinking about the fact that, however terrible
the storms may be, if one's life has a sufficiently stable and
fruitful structure, one is helped to withstand their devastating aftereffects. For most people their job does this—provides
a saving routine in time of stress. I have to create my own to
survive. And now it is time to fetch the mail and get the car
started.

January 13th

THE WOLF MOON last night, and it is well named, so bright reflecting on the glazed snow all around that I couldn't sleep. I got up three or four times to look at the thermometer—ten below zero at three A.M. I went back to bed, but felt rather panicky about pipes possibly freezing, so got up again to run water from all the taps. Just as I had fallen asleep, around four, I suppose, there was a huge thump and one of those nameless creatures who alarm the night began scrabbling around on the cellar stairs. I try to believe it is a chipmunk or large mouse and not a rat! I rarely sleep through a night alone here, but some of most fruitful thinking times are when I wake after sleeping a few hours, and in the seamless time when nothing needs to be done, not even getting up, I meditate. Last night was not easy, with the cold moon-glare outside and my harsh thoughts toward my anger. The full horror of these storms is, of course, the harm they do to those one loves. For days afterward I am forced to try to come to terms with myself and to face the destroyer and breaker in me. I do not feel remorse so much as shame.

I still feel bruised by that *Times* review. It did throw me off balance. It was like being tripped and thrown to the ground just as one has started a race to win.

These days X complains a lot about the job. By comparison my "job" must seem easy, my whole way of life self-in-

dulgent. And in some ways it is. When we have been
together for a week, and then tear apart and each go back to
his own life, in an obscure, irrational way we each resent the
differences.

January 16th

THIS HAS BEEN a bad week. I have accomplished next to
nothing, wasted time . . . and been depressed. A luncheon on
Wednesday did not help. Lunches are just not good. They
take the heart out of the day and the spaciousness from the
morning's work. Add to this extreme cold that saps energy. I
can feel it draining out like sand when I go out for a few
minutes to fill bird feeders or struggle to get the car started.

January 17th

TWENTY BELOW ZERO when I got up at seven. Even the cosy
room was below seventy (thermostat set at eighty) and I
was so afraid Punch might die of cold that the first thing I
did was to make a fire in there; I had breakfast in there
myself to keep warm too. Besides, it is a cheering thing to

take the lid off Punch's cage and hear his screams of delight
to be "out," and then his tender remarks as he meets himself
in the mirror. He is quite a good watchdog or "watchparrot,"
as this is the hour when neighborhood dogs come by on their
morning errands. Punch swears very crossly whenever one
enters the garden.

It is now nine. I've made my bed with clean sheets,
peeled potatoes and parboiled them, shelled peas, and got
things under way for Sunday dinner, as K. Martin is coming
over.

Just as I was writing my grim assessment of last week,
yesterday before supper, a car drove up and I was handed a
box of daffodils, blue flags, and pussy willows, plus three
yellow roses for good measure, from Anne Woodson, dear
thing, to rejoice that *A Grain of Mustard Seed*, the new book
of poems, is here. The book came yesterday and added to the
uncentered dispersions, for, of course, I had to wrap first
copies to send to friends. I felt let down to be alone with this
newborn babe, to have no one to whom I could show it. I
picked it up and tasted it here or there ... an odd book, for
an odd time, the devastating sixties of the assassinations and
the grinding down of hope about the war, the ghettos, the
unemployed, all that plagues and haunts us.

It is beautiful to have spring flowers in the house when
it's so terribly cold outside—a glittering day, the sky has the
piercing blue of the stained-glass windows at Chartres. The
sun lays long bands of light on the floors, but the chill creeps
in. I find the cold exhausting.

January 18th

A LITTLE WARMER this morning, zero instead of twenty below. With an extra blanket over the electric blanket I slept in warmth, less shivery round the edges than the night before. I slept and woke and thought about this journal. There are obviously certain themes that recur and must be continuously explored. Around them, over the years, I have accumulated the wisdom of other minds. I do not want this to turn into a commonplace book, but when it is a matter of touchstones, it may be appropriate now and then to draw on this store. So I have just spent nearly an hour trying to track down a marvelous passage in Flannery O'Connor's *The Artificial Nigger*. Countless times in these past years it has helped me move from shame after anger to the sense that one has to forgive oneself, to that moment on one's knees when the tears of relief pour down. I feel convinced that salvation like creation is a continuum, and by an act of grace we are given to enter into it, even when we feel we are beyond the pale, perhaps most of all then. This is the passage:

> Mr. Head stood very still and felt the action of mercy touch him again but this time he knew that there were no words in the world that could name it. He understood that it grew out of agony, which is not denied to any man and which is given in strange ways

to children. He understood it was all a man could carry into death to give his Maker and he suddenly burned with shame that he had so little of it to take with him. He stood appalled, judging himself with the thoroughness of God, while the action of mercy covered his pride like a flame and consumed it. He had never thought himself a great sinner before but he saw now that his true depravity had been hidden from him lest it cause him despair. He realized that he was forgiven for sins from the beginning of time, when he had conceived in his own heart the sin of Adam, until the present, when he had denied poor Nelson. He saw that no sin was too monstrous for him to claim as his own, and since God loved in proportion as He forgave, he felt ready at that instant to enter Paradise.

A strange empty day. I did not feel well, lay around, looked at daffodils against the white walls, and twice thought I must be having hallucinations because of their extraordinary scent that goes from room to room. I always forget how important the empty days are, how important it may be sometimes not to expect to produce anything, even a few lines in a journal. I am still pursued by a neurosis about work inherited from my father. A day where one has not pushed oneself to the limit seems a damaged damaging day, a sinful day. Not so! The most valuable thing we can do for the psyche, occasionally, is to let it rest, wander, live in the changing light of a room, not try to be or do anything whatever. Tonight I do feel in a state of grace, limbered up, less strained. Before supper I was able to begin to sort out poems of the last two years ... there is quite a bunch. For my sixtieth birthday I intend to publish sixty new poems and, as I see it now, it will be a book of chiefly love poems. *Sixty at Sixty*, I call it, for fun.

January 19th

TEN BELOW TODAY, and still the glittering, stained-glass blue sky that looks relentless now. I long for the shift that will come any day to a warmer air and snow, gentle snow.

How unnatural the imposed view, imposed by a puritanical ethos, that passionate love belongs only to the young, that people are dead from the neck down by the time they are forty, and that any deep feeling, any passion after that age, is either ludicrous or revolting! The French have always known that our capacity for loving mellows and ripens, and love if it is any good at all gets better with age. Perhaps it is not the puritan in us who has spread this myth. Perhaps it is just the opposite; the revolt against puritanism has opened up a new ethos where sex is the god, and thus the sexual athlete is the true hero. Here the middle-aged or old are at a disadvantage. Where we have the advantage is in loving itself—we know so much more; we are so much better able to handle anxiety, frustration, or even our own romanticism; and deep down we have such a store of tenderness. These should be the Mozartian years.

On the surface my work has not looked radical, but perhaps it will be seen eventually that in a "nice, quiet, noisy way" I have been trying to say radical things gently so that they may penetrate without shock. The fear of homosexuality is so great that it took courage to write *Mrs. Stevens,** to

---

* *Mrs. Stevens Hears the Mermaids Singing.*

write a novel about a woman homosexual who is not a sex maniac, a drunkard, a drug-taker, or in any way repulsive; to portray a homosexual who is neither pitiable nor disgusting, without sentimentality; and to face the truth that such a life is rarely happy, a life where art must become the primary motivation, for love is never going to fulfill in the usual sense.

But I am well aware that I probably could not have "leveled" as I did in that book had I had any family (my parents were dead when I wrote it), and perhaps not if I had had a regular job. I have a great responsibility because I can afford to be honest. The danger is that if you are placed in a sexual context people will read your work from a distorting angle of vision. I did not write *Mrs. Stevens* until I had written several novels concerned with marriage and with family life.

"How do you know so much about marriage?" How many people have asked me that question lately! The nostalgia for family life partly explains it, the nostalgia of the only child for whom what appears to most people as "ordinary" is romantic in the extreme. As a child I was always borrowing other people's families, being invited for a week or a month in the summer to share a family life—with the Boutons in Kearsarge, with the Copley Greenes in Rowley, with the Runkles in Duxbury, and above all with the Limboschs outside Brussels, in Belgium. But it was not in these families that I learned much about marriage or consciously observed it—the parents were shadowy figures in their relation to each other; it was their relation to us children that mattered to us then. No, I learned about marriage from my parents and their good, fruitful, but painful and not complete marriage, and from my own private life and the men and women whom I have loved.

I suppose what all this comes down to is that the American ethos is still fundamentally puritanical (whatever I said above) and its values based not on a flowering of life or anything like that, but on restrictions, disciplines, mores that have to be questioned before any human being can become fully human. And it is just this questioning that is now cracking this society in a healthy way, as the young batter their way through to a new ethos. The process seems often chaotic and even violent, but eventually we have to find an ethos that includes stability and harmony, for growth is not possible without them. My mail is full of cries of hunger and they are really cries of hunger for experience in the deep and fulfilling sense of the word. If a woman has artificial flowers in her house, flowers that need dusting twice a year but never die, she is closing herself off from any understanding of death. And if a woman has to remain thirty-nine, she is arresting her own growth as surely as if she were a Chinese lady a hundred years ago and had bound her feet.

The other day I was sent a novel in galleys that has proved disturbing. It is about four women in their fifties living in apartments on four floors of an old house in New York City. In each case sex plays a predominant part in the life, but it is handled so crudely and the women portrayed are so without a modicum of "sensibility" that I wonder whether the book was not written by a man under a pseudonym. Not one of them loves anyone but herself, and all are obsessed by the crude act of sex per se! The author might have got away with one such person, but four suggests a misogynist. If not a man, the author of this horrible novel must be very young, so young that she conceives of late middle age as *monstrous*. I wrote the publishers a very rude letter about the book.

When I speak of life and love as expanding with age, sex

seems the least important thing. At any age we grow by the enlarging of consciousness, by learning a new language, or a new art or craft (gardening?) that implies a new way of looking at the universe. Love is one of the great enlargers of the person because it requires us to "take in" the stranger and to understand him, and to exercise restraint and tolerance as well as imagination to make the relationship work. If love includes passion, it is more explosive and dangerous and forces us to go deeper. Great art does the same thing ... Rilke's "Archaic Torso of Apollo":

> Here there is nothing that does not see you.
> You must change your life.

January 27th

BACK FROM a weekend away with X in the middle of a true January thaw. But last night the temperature dropped by thirty-five degrees in a few hours and the world froze stiff again. It is now, at half past four, below zero and the wind truly cruel. The chickadees look so very frail, their puffballs of feathers blown every which way. I have a fire burning in the study and Grand Soleil d'Or narcissus out in a bowl on my desk. Their scent, between lemon and something sweeter and more tropical, haunts the air. I planted daffodils in several pots this afternoon, and have put two amaryllis on the window sill, but I fear it may be too cold to get them started properly.

The wild cat has come back and now miaows. Before, she stared at me with her green eyes and waited in silence. I gave her milk and meat, but when I went to take the dishes in the milk had frozen, only half finished. She did finish the meat in time. I wish I could persuade her to come in, but she is far too wild—runs away when I put the dish down and waits till I am out of sight before she will taste anything.

Loneliness is with me. It was awful coming back to the empty house, where so much needs doing. At least Win French had finished the long bench I designed for the storeroom. It looks splendid, four big bins for storing odds and ends. How wonderful it is to have a neighbor who can build such a thing!

Only the air around me feels dead. I cannot animate my life these days. I feel marooned here. Spent the entire morning sorting out my desk, making long-distance calls about lectures, about income tax (my usual panic), and for a while the phone was out of order—a day of small agitations and small anxieties that devoured my peace. I feel stupid and cross this evening.

It occurs to me that boredom and panic are the two devils the solitary must combat. When I lay down this afternoon, I could not rest and finally got up because I was in a sweat of panic, panic for no definable reason, a panic of solitude, I presume.

I am bored with my life here at present. There is not enough nourishment in it. There are times when the lack of any good conversation, theatre, concerts, art museums around here—cultured life—creates a vacuum of boredom.

And, as I have said many times to X, the real problem is that the adventure of coming to Nelson alone is over now and I simply maintain what I was once busy creating.

I feel old, dull, and useless.

January 28th

THE COLD is numbing. I was terrified this morning that Punch might not have survived, as I can't get the house over sixty-two these bitterly cold nights, but he seemed cheerful when I took the cage cover off. Now I am going to try an electric blanket as cover; that should keep him warm as toast.

I have just answered letters about *Kinds of Love* from Oregon, California, Pennsylvania, and Indiana. I would love to know how each of these people got hold of it, how they discovered its existence. It has never been reviewed in *Saturday Review*, for instance.

February 1st

TEN BELOW AGAIN this morning, but I slept well, knowing
that Punch was safe and warm. The electric blanket has
proved an excellent device. I woke several times and wandered about the house, checking taps to be sure the pipes
had not frozen and stopping to think. The stars were huge,
like daisies through the windowpanes.

I have only to imagine what it would be like were these
very quiet days, under no immediate pressure, taken from
me to realize how precious they are. Yesterday afternoon the
light in the cosy room was beautiful, marbling the cupboard
by the fireplace as I have seen it every year at this time,
turning the hills across the meadow deep rose at sunset,
making long shadows across the snow below every tree
trunk. It was a tender light, gentler, no longer the relentless
brilliance of January. And of course it is marvelous to have
the sun go down an hour or so later at last.

The other day a friend was robbed (when she was out of
town) of everything of value in her house from TV to
antique glass and china and *every* lamp, including valuable
shades. She spoke of the sense of attack, of the horror of the
times, all that "loose hostility." The attack was not personal
(I presume not, anyway) but it feels as if it had been. Probably the thieves were on drugs, and the wonder is that houses
are not broken into more often around here. I am somewhat
protected by being in the village, also by the fact that I have

no American antiques; that is what thieves are after. Yet in these last three years I have felt fear for the first time in this house, the fear of the stranger of ill will who may knock on the door or smash a window to get in.

The postal strike in Britain has been going on now for more than two weeks and it is strange not to be able to communicate with friends and relatives there. My cousin, Janet, sent me three books of poems for Christmas. How delighted I am to plunge again into Arthur Waley's translations from the Chinese! Reading them, feeling the power of direct description and how it affects the reader's mood, I dreamed in the night of writing some poems of quiet happiness, descriptions of shadow on snow or light on the walls of a room. Will it be possible? Or is poetry for me always a matter of handling tension, a polarity between tensions?

Janet sent also Ted Hughes's *Crow*. There is a fashion at present (Berryman began it) for finding a persona of this sort, an outrageous, dark, humorous, awkward persona into which anxiety, rage, and crazy laughter can be poured. We are tired of being ourselves, naked—is that it? Women do not feel the need of a persona, but I have an idea that women are far more interested in self-actualization than men are. Women internalize their lives to a greater extent, and the poetry of internalization can be valid. Form may create the necessary "distance." What bothers me is nakedness as bravado. Then it becomes embarrassing: "Look at me ... Aren't I shocking?" But transparency does not shock: "Look through me and find everyman, yourself." Somewhere between the minute particular and the essence lies the land of poetry.

But as I write this I hear no roar of the waves, feel no undertow dragging me under into the fertile unconscious world of creation.

February 2nd

I'VE BEEN up and down like mercury this morning. Woke feeling grippey, with a headache, nausea. But the sky is so radiantly blue, the sunlight so powerful an element this morning that as I lay in bed for half an hour after breakfast I felt life flow back in like brandy. I felt excited, trembling, at the thought of all I have to say here and of poems to be—gently shifting patterns like seaweed in the ocean of my mind as I lay there—and finally I had the strength to get up and bring in pine wood (at seven that had seemed an impossible task). Again the long, flowing horizontal lines of tree shadows made me stop at the kitchen sink and just look for a few minutes.

It is nearly impossible to visualize the summer when we are in this strongly defined black and white and blue world of the winter, to visualize how the distant hills disappear behind the trees, how it all finally becomes an enclosing jungle of leaves. All this white against all that green! In some ways I love the winter best—the relief of not having to garden! The austerity and brilliance of it, such as one experiences also on a bright day at the seashore. And for the same reasons it is, at times, tiring.

A good piece by Auden in the *Times*. I read it while eating a hot dog at the kitchen counter and felt happy. His theme is that we are losing two precious qualities, the ability to laugh heartily and the ability to pray, a plea for carnival and for prayer, the conscious thumbing of the nose at death. I suppose that the only prayer—reached only *after* all pleas for grace or for some specific gift have been uttered and laid aside—is, "Give me to be in your presence." This is really just about what George Harrison, the Beatle, sings in the hit song of the moment: "I want to know you, I want to be with you." Simone Weil says, "Absolute attention is prayer." And the more I have thought about this over the years, the truer it is for me. I have used the sentence often in talking about poetry to students, to suggest that if one looks long enough at almost anything, looks with absolute attention at a flower, a stone, the bark of a tree, grass, snow, a cloud, something like revelation takes place. Something is "given," and perhaps that something is always a reality *outside* the self. We are aware of God only when we cease to be aware of ourselves, not in the negative sense of denying the self, but in the sense of losing self in admiration and joy.

And in a strange way laughter has the same effect. We are able to laugh when we achieve detachment, if only for a moment.

What a mystery Auden is! He has made a new kind of poetry, far more original even than Eliot, I think, a kind of poetry based on the antithesis of the "poetic" as we used to know it, never inflated, ironic, antiromantic, witty. And all of this could stem from Byron, but Auden has his own vision. "Lay your sleeping head, my love/Human on my faithless arm"—I can remember how the lines enraged me when I first read them. But I was wrong. Auden has been rarely *honest*, and being honest is harder than it looks if the self admits to being homosexual. He has not indulged in the romantic view (which can take the form of perdition, as in Burroughs, or in false glamourizing). We all do make some attempt to bring together the private and the public person through the work of art. It is possible now in a way that it was not before.

February 4th

I WOKE to the sun on a daffodil. I had put a bunch of daffodils and purple tulips on the bureau and when I woke the sun hit just one daffodil, a single beam on the yellow frilled cup and outer petals. After a bad night that sight got me up and going.

I had gone to bed in tears the night before, one of those fits of hysterical weeping after a day of frustrations and irritating demands, one from an old lady begging me to come to see her. I should do it, but I don't really like her and am afraid of getting caught. She has been insistent before and has no idea, of course, how badgered I am. I felt like a criminal to say No again; finally sent her *Kinds of Love* as a post-birthday present. By then the thread of the morning's work was broken and I never got back to my center. Hurried off to Keene to shop for food and picked up flowers that someone had ordered because I told her I was in a doldrum, not someone I know at all well. So I felt embarrassed, another failing of mine in telling people too much, although a doldrum is hardly a depression. Was horrified at what I paid for a weekend's food and liquor when people are starving.

I did write a poem, so it was not a wholly wasted day, after all. And it occurs to me that there is a proper balance between not asking enough of oneself and asking or expecting too much. It may be that I set my sights too high and so repeatedly end a day in depression. Not easy to find the balance, for if one does not have wild dreams of achievement, there is no spur even to get the dishes washed. One must think like a hero to behave like a merely decent human being.

But there is another reason for a dark mood. I thought I was approaching the publication of the new poems, *A Grain of Mustard Seed,* in perfect calm, accepting that there will be no review of consequence, glad simply to be able to give it to my friends. I have waited three weeks for paperbacks to send out, so few friends have seen it, and even friends find it hard to respond to poetry.

Jung says, "The serious problems in life are never fully solved. If ever they should appear to be so it is a sure sign that something has been lost. The meaning and purpose of a problem seem to lie not in its solution but in our working at it incessantly. This alone preserves us from stultification and petrefaction." And so, no doubt, with the problems of a solitary life.

After I had looked for a while at that daffodil before I got up, I asked myself the question, "What do you want of your life?" and I realized with a start of recognition and terror, "Exactly what I have—but to be commensurate, to handle it all better."

Yet it is not those fits of weeping that are destructive. They clear the air, as Herbert says so beautifully:

> Poets have wronged poor storms: such days are best;
> They purge the air without, within the breast.

What is destructive is impatience, haste, expecting too much too fast.

February 5th

It is snowing hard, a blizzard. What a relief it is after the cruel shining of these past weeks, how gentle and enclosing! It has become exhausting to live as we did in the center of a diamond, light reflected from snow, and no shade or shelter. The relentless blue sky, the relentless cold ended by having a curious flatness. One could not respond.

Yesterday I accomplished one big task, clearing out the cupboard by the fireplace in the cosy room, where I have stuffed paper and boxes for years. I filled all the trash cans and then had to use plastic trash bags, but at last it is done. In a cigar box I found a dead mouse, perfect, sitting as if stuffed on the most beautiful nest (just like a bird's nest) made of bits of wool and string and lined with something white and soft. It was poignant to think that she must have made the nest and prepared to give birth and then, no doubt, was poisoned. She had a white belly and a very sweet face, a field mouse. They come in every autumn in droves since the cats are with Judy in winter. The smell was awful. I finally lighted some piñon incense someone sent for Christmas, and that did help. Now I feel a sense of relief when I walk past that cupboard and know it is neat and in order.

There are times when I find myself going back to Louis Lavelle's *Le Mal et la Souffrance*. The second chapter of this remarkable book is called "Tous les Etres Séparés et Unis" and it is this that has nourished and reassured me in my own belief that solitude is one of the ways toward communion. He says:

> We sense that there can be no true communion between human beings until they have in fact become beings: for to be able to give oneself one must have taken possession of oneself in that painful solitude outside of which nothing belongs to us and we have nothing to give. . . . And one might even say that I begin to communicate with others as soon as I begin to communicate with myself. So true it is that the most tragic solitude is that which keeps me from forcing the barrier between what I think I am from what I am: because then my consciousness has become such a stranger to my true self and my distress is so great that I can no longer say what I desire nor what I lack. Solitude is to feel the presence in oneself of a power that cannot act, but which, as soon as it is able to, obliges me to realize myself by multiplying my relations with myself and with all human beings.
>
> Nevertheless this solitude into which we have just come, and which gives us such a strong sense of inner responsibility, and at the same time of the impossibility of being self-sufficient, is experienced as a solitude only because it is at the same time an appeal toward solitudes like our own with whom we feel the need to be in communion; for it is only through this communion that each consciousness will discover the essence of its destiny which is not to perceive things or to dominate them, but is to live, and that means to find outside itself other consciousnesses from which it never stops receiving and to whom it never stops giving in an uninterrupted circuit of light, of joy and of love, which is the only law of the spiritual universe.

Photo by Mort Mace

February 8th

ELEANOR BLAIR for overnight in a lovely interval of warmer weather and sunshine on Saturday. I have not had a guest here since January 6th, even for an hour or two, so it was quite an event. I enjoyed getting ready—tea and a fire to welcome her when she arrived. I could look at the house again not as a disintegrating machine to keep going by a daily effort but as a lovely shelter in which to welcome a guest. Eleanor notices everything, is more than anyone the "friend of the work." (How she helped me by typing, editing, and believing in *Kinds of Love* during the long struggle to get it done!)

On Sunday morning we went for a walk, my first walk since before Christmas—it has been too cold—across the green and then a quarter mile or so up to the French farm. Lovely to smell a springlike air and to hear the two spring notes of the chickadees for the first time. The jays too have their somewhat musical spring cry (it cannot be called a song, I fear). Halfway up the hill we were greeted by Pixie, that exquisite sprite of a sheltie, and by one of the beagles, and by a faint sound of lambs baaing in the barn. But when we arrived, we found sheep and lambs outdoors, the lambs leaping in the air, the sheep eating snow greedily as if it were caviar. I held one black lamb in my arms and felt the soft nose nuzzling my cheek. Such fine soft wool too! There they were, a marvelous congregation of cats, dogs, sheep, lambs, kittens, and Cathy going back and forth to supervise her flock. The fourteenth lamb was being born on the instant and I rushed into the barn, hoping to hear again the extraordinary throaty, hungry sound the mother makes when she licks her lamb for the first time. This sheep was silent, but it is always moving to watch Cathy and her expert hands as she leads the lamb to the tits. This child, now perhaps fifteen, started off with a pet lamb when she was only five or six and has become a true shepherd with a flock of twenty or thirty, a ram, and a yearly yield of twenty or more. And this is only part of the marvelous world Dot and Win have created for their children, a "peaceable kingdom." All the years I have been here it has been a joy to watch the little boy and his absolute confidence with all animals. The atmosphere of the place is enhanced by its site, at the top of a hill, out of the sheltered bowl where the village center lies. Here there is open space, a great view over surrounding hills, today purplish and velvety against an ominous sky. As the shifting clouds crossed the sun, the sun looked like the moon, and I was glad for Eleanor's sake that she would be home before the storm.

It did give me a shivery feeling as to what was going to happen next in this wild wintry world. It was a tempestuous night, high winds howling about the eaves, and a mixture of rain and snow pattering against the windows. I wondered what I would find when I woke, but when I did, Win French was driving up with the plough and I could see we had been let off easy with only about three inches. Because of the high wind it has drifted here and there. Mildred is here cleaning now.

I am so glad I don't have to go out. A whole day before me in which to think and be!

February 9th

IT IS RATHER like living in a vast cosmic mood-swing here now. I managed to get the car out yesterday and did some quick errands because another storm was in the air. It came, all right, with strong wind, snow, then lashing rain, temperature just above freezing. I woke to trees iced in silver and an April sky, sunlight breaking through clouds. Now in the last half hour it has suddenly become ominously dark, all clouded over, the clouds nearly black. The wind is back.

And it is the same inside me—violent mood-swings. It would be a real deprivation to have no phone here, but on the other hand how devastating a voice can be! I feel myself sucked down into the quicksand that isolation sometimes creates, a sense of drowning, of being literally *engulfed*. When it comes to the important things one is always alone, and it may be that the virtue or possible insight I get from being so obviously alone—being physically and in every way absolutely alone much of the time—is a way into the universal state of man. The way in which one handles this absolute aloneness is the way in which one grows up, is the great psychic journey of everyman. At what price would total independence be bought? That's the the rub! I am conscious of the fruitful tension set up between me and anyone for whom I care—Anne Woodson for instance, X of course. I learn by being *in relation to*.

When one is alone a lot as I am, this becomes true even
of such an apparently passive relation as that between me
and four bowls of daffodils I am growing on the window sill
of the guest room. Whether or not a flower or plant is doing
well becomes of singular importance. When I get up in the
morning, it matters what tone of voice Punch uses. A happy
scream as I lift the lid off the cage and he is free to climb out
and sit on a rod outside to admire himself in a mirror makes
me laugh with joy. When he is silent, as he was today, I feel
it, as I feel for the wild cat who will never be tamed, I fear,
but comes every afternoon for milk and food and stares at
me intently with her round green eyes. I have wept with
anxiety more than once when she was not there. It is absurd.
Yet how, without such intimate relations, keep alive at all?
Every relation challenges; every relation asks me to be something, do something, respond. Close off response and what is
left? Bearing ... enduring ... waiting.

The sun has suddenly come out and there is a bright blue
sky—all this happened while I wrote a few words! Astonish-
ing!

I have begun again to play two Schubert Impromptus
that Louise Bogan gave me—Opus 90 and Opus 142, Giese-
king.

I have said elsewhere that we have to make myths of our
lives, the point being that if we do, then every grief or
inexplicable seizure by weather, woe, or work can—if we discipline ourselves and think hard enough—be turned to
account, be made to yield further insight into what it is to be
alive, to be a human being, what the hazards are of a fairly
usual, everyday kind. We go up to Heaven and down to Hell
a dozen times a day—at least, I do. And the discipline of
work provides an exercise bar, so that the wild, irrational

motions of the soul become formal and creative. It literally keeps one from falling on one's face.

That is one way to keep alive in self-made solitary confinement. I have found it useful also these past days to say to myself, "What if I were not alone? What if I had ten children to get off to school every morning and a massive wash to do before they got home? What if two of them were in bed with flu, cross and at a loose end?" That is enough to send me back to solitude as if it were—as it truly is—a fabulous gift from the gods.

Contrast is one key, and within every day the deliberate creation of diversity. This morning I cheered myself out of depression by saying, "Your reward for the morning's work will be to clean out the liquor cupboard." It is a mess, but a viable mess compared to that of the paper cupboard, despite the rat poison strewn around because I saw a huge rat crawl up the wall in there one day.

Each day, and the living of it, has to be a conscious creation in which discipline and order are relieved with some play and some pure foolishness. God bless Punch, who makes me laugh aloud!

My greatest deprivation is to have no huggable animal around. I miss the two old cats dreadfully.

February 13th

THE HOUSE is full of spring flowers, valentines. There is no month when I can imagine spring flowers being more of a delight. Yesterday the trees were sheathed in ice and it is bitterly cold; so the freshness, the aliveness of daffodils and iris and tulips indoors is quite overwhelming. Even the rich green leaves and the scent in this frozen odorless world seem like marvels.

I have been pondering two passage from Jung. The first is a key to the dangers of sublimation: "One does not become enlightened by imagining figures of light, but by making the darkness conscious." The second is:

> Only the living presence of the eternal images can lend the human psyche a dignity that makes it morally possible for a man to stand by his own soul, and be convinced that it is worth his while to persevere with himself. Only then will he realize that the conflict is in *him*, that the discord and tribulation are his riches, which should not be squandered by attacking others; and that if fate should exact a debt from him in the form of guilt, it is a debt to himself.

February 22nd

STRANGE to come back to this white world after a weekend away in Norfolk, Virginia, where I read poems, and then twenty-four hours in Washington, staying with Margaret Bouton. It is wonderful to stay with her because I can spend hours in the National Gallery, where she is a curator, while she works in her office. This time I went back to the Flemish painters with renewed devotion and afterward by a great piece of luck saw Kenneth Clark's synthesis on the period, "The Light of Experience."

Near the Flemish painters hangs a small Clouet that seems to communicate the essence of French refinement and *clarté*. But the Flemish painters are in my blood. It is the combination of the restless skies and the homely interiors, the way light moves about the Dutch rooms, not only in Vermeer (Vermeer, of course!) but even in Pieter de Hooch that touches me deeply. A still life by Culp gave me a moment of absolute joy—a cut lemon, light on two wineglasses. I was struck later in a Rembrandt portrait by the contrast between the rough bold strokes with which the face was painted, as if to make its troubled humanity clear, and the delicacy of the rendering of the lace collar and suit. I suppose these paintings speak to me with such force because they represent all that I hope to do in the novels and in the poems. They compose the world without ever imposing a rigid schema upon it and make us see even the domestic scene at its most banal with a sudden sense of revelation, with poignant recognition. The painters look at reality with devotion, and what we see is life never sentimentalized, but enhanced.

Under all these pleasures, including a delightful dinner party Margaret gave for me—stirring talk with three brilliant men (how starved I have been for that!)—under it all were my thoughts about *Modern Woman, The Lost Sex,* Marynia F. Farnham. Reading the book is and is meant to be a deeply disturbing experience. The picture it draws of a totally disoriented and neurotic civilization acts upon any reader like an earthquake. This book is least convincing in certain categorical statements about men and women; also, a bias in the metaphors appears to demand analysis, for they struck me as being consistently pejorative where women are concerned. (Perhaps it should have been vetted by another psychoanalyst!) Naturally I objected violently to a statement which predicates that "authentic" genius makes its appearance only in a heterosexual male, with Bach as the great prototype. A differentiation is thus made between what the author calls "compensatory" genius and "authentic" genius. Formulas about genius never work for me, and always arouse distaste and even anger because human beings are so much more complex and diverse in their means of self-actualization than any category can permit. I cannot believe that a definition that excludes Michelangelo, Tolstoi, Dickens, Mozart, Cézanne, and God knows how many more neurotic, or unmarried, or homosexual men and women can be taken seriously! It is significant that the "authentic" geniuses held up as exemplars were either musical or mathematical, modes of genius that show themselves early, even before puberty. In literature and painting it is altogether different. I would predicate that in all great works of genius masculine and feminine elements in the personality find expression, whether this androgynous nature is played out sexually or not. Thomas Mann is a good example. And, at a much lower level of genius, Vita Sackville-West.

There are many insights in *Modern Woman* that I can go along with wholly. For years, for instance, I have lamented the devaluation of the nursing profession because nurturing is woman's work and uses her special genius. It is tragic that blacks in their struggle for self-definition have come to regard this profession as *menial* (like housework) and discriminatory. We have so much to learn from them about grace and instinct, intuitive understanding of what the sick and vulnerable need. They have natural warmth. I remember Robert Klopstock's telling me that he always asked for black nurses after a lobectomy.

But what is becoming tiresome now in the American ethos is the emphasis on sex, and especially on orgasm as an end in itself. Let us think more about what enriches life; to put it in metaphorical form, let us think about flowers and animals in a new way. A sensitized person who feels himself at peace with nature and with the natural man in him is not going to be troubled about sex. It will have its day and its hour and the orgasm, should it occur, will come not as a little trick cleverly performed, but as a wave of union with the whole universe. The emphasis on orgasm per se is just another example of the devaluation of all that is human.

I am furious at all the letters to answer, when all I want to do is think and write poems. A strange time, when violent things are taking place in the psyche. I long for open time, with no obligations except toward the inner world and what is going on there. But when so much is and must be unre-

solved, perhaps silence is just as well. Anyway, it is now
noon and I have kept at the letters doggedly since nine.

How sad and empty the house felt when I walked in yesterday afternoon! Even Punch, poor dear, is subdued by days
of solitude, though Mildred comes faithfully to wake and
feed him and to put him to bed. A few days of neglect and
the soul goes out of the house, that's sure.

March 1st

AND NOW the great spring skies are here, the more dazzling
because the snow is still three feet or more deep all around.
But there is a lift in the air, in the spring notes of the jays
and chickadees, in the stirring of sap in maples and in me. I
feel hugely happy, in a state of bliss after a wonderful weekend with X that included a long windy walk by the sea. I got
back yesterday as the sun was setting, pouring golden light
on the snow and lighting up the white walls. For once I did
not feel the pang of the empty house. It welcomed me, and
after an hour (I had been watching for her) the wild cat
came and I fed her. It set a seal on all I had been feeling, for
there is no doubt that this shy, intense, starved creature has
become an alter ego. I have identified with the perpetual
hungerer after comfort, the outsider watching lighted windows.

I feel sometimes like a house with no walls. The mood is
caught in a photo Mort Mace took of this house all lighted

up one March evening. The effect is dazzling from the outside, just as my life *seems* dazzling to many people in its
productivity, in what it communicates that is human and fulfilled, and hence fulfilling. But the truth is that whatever
good effect my work may have comes, rather, from my own
sense of isolation and vulnerability. The house *is* open in a
way that no house where a family lives and interacts can be.
My life, often frightfully lonely, interacts with a whole lot of
people I do not know and will never know. What they sense
is what Gide calls *"un être disponible,"* available because of
my isolation, because I have no family. I often think of Isak
Dinesen's motto, one she invented after the death of Denys
Fitz-Hatton: *"Je réponderai."* It has been my device for
many years, a rule of conduct. But that capacity, that necessity to answer, ceases to exist when I am too absorbed in my
own never-solved problems. It is poetry, then, that lights up
the house, as in Mort's photograph. I am a little sad now
because, for the moment, poetry is not here.

March 3rd

ONE OF THE BLESSINGS of my life here is that I can wake up
naturally, lie, and think, before being precipitated into the
day. The subconscious flows gently through that first consciousness, remembering, putting out feelers toward the
weather. I nearly always get up between six thirty and seven
thirty; there is no great difference between one day and

another, but the fact that I have leeway, that nothing need be forced, makes the difference.

Today, an iron-gray world. After breakfast I filled the feeders and emptied wastebaskets because we are sure to have a blizzard. It has been announced; the wind is from the northeast, and when I came in, I felt snow on my face. Now it is snowing in earnest. Another wonderful day enclosed in my cocoon. Today I hope to write a poem—so much has been precipitated in my mind lately and nothing yet settled.

In the night I remembered a Greek myth that tells of two lovers, one who loved only the mountains and the other only the sea; so they had to meet between the two or not at all. Thinking about it brought back Millay's poem "Mist in the Valley," which ends:

Stricken too sore for tears,
I stand, remembering the islands and the sea's lost sound. . . .
Life at its best no longer than the sand-peep's cry,
And I two years, two years,
Tilling an upland ground!

How often I have felt that here, setting images of the sea here and there—a shell on a mantel and, of course, the Hokusai in the big room.

What a fine musical invention the poems of Millay are where she alternates, rather roughly, apparently naturally on the breath itself, long lines with short ones . . . perfect in "The Buck in the Snow." Too often she is a weak echo of Housman or Shakespeare. And in the end, alas, she was not able to create a viable structure—either within herself or in the poems—for maturity.

Yesterday I had a beautiful letter from Eugénie about old age (she is in her seventies).

Ici la vie continue égale et monotone en surface, pleine d'éclairs, de sommets et de désepérance, dans les profondeurs. Nous sommes arrivés maintenant à un stade de vie si riche en appréhensions nouvelles intransmissibles aux autres âges de la vie—on se sent rempli à la fois de tant de douceur et de tant de désespoir—l'énigme de cette vie grandit, grandit, vous submerge et vous écrase, puis tout à coup en une lueur suprême on prend conscience du "sacré."

Here life goes on, even and monotonous on the surface, full of lightning, of summits and of despair, in its depths. We have now arrived at a stage in life so rich in new perceptions that cannot be transmitted to those at another stage—one feels at the same time full of so much gentleness and so much despair—the enigma of this life grows, grows, drowns one and crushes one, then all of a sudden in a supreme moment of light one becomes aware of the "sacred."

We have to live as close as possible to all that leaves the door open to what E means by the "holy." More and more I see how true is the Hindu idea that a man may leave family and responsibilities and become a "holy" man, a wanderer, in old age, in order to complete himself—a time for laying aside all that has pulled the soul away from nature, from pure contemplation. The problem is not to sink into apathy. The chores, the household tasks, do provide a kind of frame, but I get more and more impatient with bothering about things. It is a bore to have to have the big floor repainted yellow. It has lasted ten years and that is a lot better than I had imagined, but now it does look worn and shabby. Yesterday I tried to get paint, but it will have to be mixed, and it all takes time, "errand time." Gardening is altogether different.

There the door is always open into the "holy"—growth, birth, death. Every flower holds the whole mystery in its short cycle, and in the garden we are never far away from death, the fertilizing, good, *creative* death.

The snow falls thick and fast. . . .

March 5th

IT IS a real northeaster. The house creaks and sighs and doors bang as the wind sizzles and creeps and then suddenly bat-. ters at the house. I am always afraid that one of the old maples will crack, but so far this time I have not heard that alarming groan that used to be so frightening those first winters.

Yesterday was a wonderful day, as I worked for four unbroken hours on a poem. It is not good enough, but soon I shall get back to it, later this morning.

In the afternoon yesterday the wild cat stood up at the porch door and mewed. I opened the door and stood behind it; she hesitated, wanted to come in, tried to summon the courage, then ran away. But after I put the milk inside the house, leaving the door open, she finally did come . . . at last! I have borne her steady look, longing to trust, for six months or more. It seemed like a great blessing to know she would be safe in this frightful storm. I put food down three or four times and it always vanished, but I saw her only as a shadow, fleeing silently at my approach. In the night she miaowed a strange miaow that I thought at first must be a male cat outside, but I now believe she is in heat. This morning she has vanished somewhere in the cellar or under the house. It is beautiful to know this wild creature is somewhere inside, invisible, leading her own life, but safe.

Outside it is a milky world, snow driving past the windows incessantly in horizontal waves. Drifts pile up under the high wind. But I am truly in Heaven. There are charming "February" daffodils out in a pale green pot on my desk, tulips on the mantel a subtle apricot color veined in yellow with dark purple hearts. I have lighted the fire in here because the wind creeps in and I feel the chill. I have Beethoven sonatas (*Pastoral* and *Les Adieux*) on the record player. And now to work!

March 16th

I'VE BEEN AWAY lecturing, only a week, but it feels like months, so much got packed into that week. Coming home means being attacked by the mountain of mail, so the return to inner life feels a bit bumpy still. I came home to a white world, shrouded in mist, milky air above the vast mounds of snow, six feet high on the way from barn to road. No flowers in the house, so it felt desolate when I walked in. The wild cat is still here. Mildred has fed her. I saw her for just a fleeting second; then she vanished, strange invisible presence.

I wanted to tell someone about my adventures, but with

no one to talk to they sort themselves out while I sleep, the chaotic mass of images gradually separated out and reduced to essence. It has been a happy week because I felt useful and because so many people came to tell me, "I have read everything you have written." It always amazes me that anyone has ever read anything of mine, so it is exceedingly heartening now to discover that somehow, little by little, the work is getting through.

In Milwaukee I witnessed a wonderful sunrise over the lake from my bedroom window at Marjorie Bitker's. First, over the flat, greenish frozen water, the horizon brimmed with a warm golden light, then changed to ruddy pink—a wide peaceful opening up as if the sky itself were a huge flower. It had snowed, so the land was all white. Finally the round red disk sprang up and light flooded over it all. A moment of great peace. It started that day well. And, in spite of all the chatter beforehand (an hour for drinks, an hour of lunch before the reading), I was able to poise myself; so I was floated and the physical effort was minimized. The audience was wonderfully attentive.

Afterward Marjorie drove me out to see Frank Lloyd Wright's Greek church, round-domed, shaped like a Greek cross inside. It had a peaceful airy wholeness that seemed the architectural equivalent of the sunrise, all serenity and amplitude. But in and around that day were an interview with the paper, a radio interview, and at seven that evening a half-hour TV interview, and by the end I felt battered.

March 18th

IT IS HARD to think back in a journal, so much happens each day. That week in the Midwest already seems far off. But what remains vivid now is the memory of the plains, a wide sadness and emptiness of dark brown ploughed land under huge skies, little pigs running, a fling of lambs, and on the last day a visit to Ethel Seybold's ancient farm . . . a farm once in her family that she has rescued from almost total dilapidation. It has such a wholesome, ancient sweetness about it. She and her sister work at it as if it were a poem. On the brink of their retirement this house has become for them *the* source of joy and adventure. The village is called Fishhook. What a feeling of frontier it all still has! I was happy to end my week there and not in a city, and to end it with students. Illinois College is not rich, but I felt the freshness and fervor of the kids very deeply. A good time.

Beside my desk I have a vermilion amaryllis in flower. When I look up at the transparent petals, veined, glowing against a dazzling blue sky, it is a shout of joy and health, the victory over winter.

Yesterday I answered a letter I have been pondering for weeks. It is the archetype of many, many others I have been sent lately. In the final paragraph the writer tells me,

> I wonder which Hell is worse—the Hell of an entirely self-motivated life, or the hell of which I feel a

part: myself struggling to come to terms with what I want to say [the writer is a painter], how I want to say it, the fear and doubt. So much holds me back. My own inertia, the choice I made ten years ago to be second in marriage, the children, my background, the place women held in my background, not only in a personal sense, but in the larger sense, in our society. Just being a woman. It is difficult. Does one give up a measure of security, and whatever else is necessary, to develop? Can one *be* within the framework of a marriage, do you think? I envy your solitude with all my heart, and your courage to live as you must.

"Can one *be* within the framework of a marriage?" It is not irresponsible women who ask that question, but often (as in this instance) women with children, caring women, who feel deeply frustrated and lost, who feel they are missing their "real lives" all the time. Has this always been true and only now are we able to admit it? And what is the solution? It is partly, no doubt, as Women's Lib has insisted, that it is time the warm nurturing powers, usually taken for granted in women, now be called out of men in equal measure. Roles should no longer be assigned on the basis of sex or of any preconceived idea of marriage, but should grow organically from the specific needs of two human beings and their capacities and gifts. The phrase "second in marriage" sounds Victorian. No partner in a love relationship (whether homo- or heterosexual) should feel that he has to give up an essential part of himself to make it viable. But the fact is that men still do rather consistently undervalue or devalue women's powers as serious contributors to civilization except as homemakers. And women, no doubt, equally devalue their own powers. But there is something wrong when solitude such as mine can be "envied" by a happily married woman with children.

Mine is not, I feel sure, the best human solution. Nor have I ever thought it was. In my case it has perhaps made possible the creation of some works of art, but certainly it has done so at a high price in emotional maturity and in happiness. What I have is space around me and time around me. How they can be achieved in a marriage is the real question. It is not an easy one to answer.

It is harder than it used to be because everything has become speeded up and overcrowded. So everything that slows us down and forces patience, everything that sets us back into the slow cycles of nature, is a help. Gardening is an instrument of grace.

It is harder than it used to be because standards of house-keeping and house-decorating have become pretentious and competitive. I don't blame children for fleeing those *House Beautiful* houses, nonshelters, dehumanized, ostentatious, rarely expressing an individual family's way of life. When I was writing a column for *Family Circle* I had planned one in praise of shabbiness. A house that does not have one worn, comfy chair in it is soulless. It all comes back to the fact that we are not asked to be perfect, only human. What a relief it is to walk into a human house!

Is it, *au fond*, that we try to control too much? Plants, for instance, humanize an interior because they can't be controlled. But one does not need to show off a house, only *live* in it, to make a true shelter and nurturing place for human needs. And that means not so much efficiency as life enhancement: a cat sitting on a table to look out, a bowl of flowering bulbs, books scattered about.

I knew when I walked in here last Sunday that this

house dies when there are no flowers. It felt desolate and I ended the day in tears, as if I had been abandoned by God. Now there are crimson tulips in one room, white and pink ones in another, and I can breathe, am full of joy and at home again.

March 20th

THE FIRST DAY of spring and we are in the midst of a wild snowstorm! When it began yesterday swarms of birds came to the feeders—first a flock of goldfinches; then I glimpsed the bright pink head of a purple finch. Now there are red-wing blackbirds and, alas, starlings. When they have gone the evenings grosbeaks and jays will have their turn. Two pairs of downy woodpeckers and one of hairies come and go all day long for suet. How empty the white world outdoors would look without all these wings!

I have had two visits from painters these last days, the Vogel-Knotts and Anne Woodson, and I have been thinking that painters are enriching friends for a poet, and vice versa. Because the medium is different there is not the slightest shadow of competition, which I fear is always there between writers. The criticism we give each other, the way we look at each other's work, is pure and full of joy, a spontaneous response. I envy painters because they can set their work up and look at it whole in a way that a writer cannot, even with a single page of prose or a poem. But how hard it must be to give up a painting! When a book appears it goes out into the world, but the writer still keeps it and can go on giving it to friends over and over again. The painting is gone forever.

I suppose I envy painters because they can meditate on

form and structure, on color and light, and not concern themselves with human torment and chaos. It is restful even to imagine expression without words.

April 6th

AFTER ANOTHER WEEK away lecturing, home at last to melting snow! There are tiny bunches of snowdrops out by the granite front steps, and a few crocuses blooming between the spruce boughs . . . too soon, I fear, to take them off, for we shall surely have more cold. Only redwing blackbirds and starlings at the feeder these days. The raccoon climbs up on the woodpile on the back porch and steals the seed cake. I saw a huge woodchuck out by the barn. Has he already eaten the first tender shoots of hollyhock? Last year he devoured them all. Finally I planted tomato plants there against the warm, weathered wood. They did well, but I missed the hollyhocks.

The brooks are unlocked at last. That rush of water, foaming over rocks, dark brown, alive, bursting into small waterfalls over boulders, that is what says "spring."

But we are promised a cold northeaster and heavy snow tomorrow, so I was wise not to have the snow tires taken off.

April 7th

A TREMENDOUS white northeaster has come roaring in as predicted. Even Punch is silent this morning and sits hunched in his cage. But for me it is exhilarating—a whole empty day to try to use well, to get out of the clutter of these last "catching-up" days and what feels like thickets of undigested experience. It is hard not to be thrown by the re-entry into solitude after a week away, for I am at once attacked by many needs; many different kinds of response are required, when all I long for is to have twenty-four hours in which to sort out what has happened to me. I feel like a river when the tide changes and for a while the waters flow in crosscurrent, with no direction, only a pulling from all sides.

It was disturbing, for instance, to find a note asking me to send my letters from Louise Bogan to her literary executor, who wants to bring out selected letters. What I have to do is open that big folder and dive down into a relationship that had great meaning for me long ago.

I shall not ever forget walking into the apartment at 137 East 168th Street for the first time, after an all-night drive from Washington. I felt a sharp pang of nostalgia as I walked into that civilized human room, filled with the light of a sensitized, bitter, lucid mind. The impact was so great because not since I walked into Jean Dominique's two rooms above the school in Brussels had I felt so much at home in my inner self. In each instance the habitation reflected in a very special way the tone, the hidden music, as it were, of a woman, and a woman living alone, the sense of a deep loam of experience and taste expressed in the surroundings, the room a shell that reverberated with oceans and tides and waves of the owner's past, the essence of a human life as it had lived itself into certain colors, *objets d'art*, and especially into many books. The nostalgia comes from the longing to be taken into that world by what the French call an *amitié amoureuse*, recognized from the start as an attraction that will never be "realized" as a love affair, but where there is a strong echo of feeling on each side, whether uttered or not—perfume on the air of sadness, renunciation even, or the light bitter taste of a persimmon. Louise's word for this atmosphere was "life-enhancing."

The substance of such relationships lies in certain affinities close to the soul—affinities that will keep the relationship nonpassionate, tender, and full of revelation.

Those rooms were inhabited by women older than I, for whom I felt homage as well as love. I have felt at home in the same way occasionally in a house or room where a marriage has flowered or where two friends (Bill and Paul's apartment in San Francisco comes to mind) live in communion. But then one is inevitably shut out from the essence. Not enough has been said of the value of a life lived alone in that it is lived in a house with an open door, with room for the stranger, for the new friend to be taken in and cherished. For Louise, Jean-Do, and for me availability had and has to be handled with delicacy or one could be swamped. Detachment must be cultivated against the longing to be perfectly open and receptive. It all comes back to poise, the poise of the soul when it is in true balance. The human mistakes I make often come from rushing in fast in order to be "done" with something, to have answered, to get it off the desk ... and this forced response may go too far, give away too much, or not selectively enough.

Whatever people I take into my life I take in because they challenge me and I challenge them at the deepest level. Such relationships are rarely serene, but they are nourishing. As I wrote the above, Kot* came vividly to mind. He would have agreed perfectly with this statement, and as I opened an old journal, I came upon parts of his letters, copied out after his death. These two showed me again what a friend he was:

> You see, I am very fond of you and I should like you to possess all virtues, without a spot or stain. You have millions of virtues, but you postpone their practice. Hence my preaching at you. But as you are not only a darling but a terribly wise being, you must listen to me seriously, although you are allowed to smile. (See what an inconsistent person I am, for the sake of your smile, I spoil my whole case.) ... I want you to be aware of what you call your "steel," and what I call your wisdom, all the time. I mean, that whatever mad or chaotic things you do, never forget that there is your ultimate wisdom that must keep you safe and whole....
>
> Of course I shall be scolding you and be terribly severe, and even beat you on occasion. And all of this out of very good and so tender love for you.

* S. S. Koteliansky.

Photo by Mort Mace

April 12th

QUITE PREPOSTEROUS that there is still snow on the ground! I always forget how maddening mud season can be. A raccoon climbs up and steals the seed cake every night if I don't remember to take it in, and I then have to search about in the snow and mud for the empty basket. At the regular feeder there are now only starlings, redwing blackbirds, and cow birds. Too stupid! And the apparition of that enormous, probably pregnant woodchuck is no help at all!

But today there is a feel of spring in the air at last, and it will be seventy by noon. In front of the house, where it is warmest, a row of crocuses have survived the big snow and are now wide open to the sun—lots of white ones, lavender striped with purple, and yellow ones. But in the storm a while back, when the grader was used to plough, massive blocks of packed snow were piled on top of the big pink Rugosa rose that I planted ten years ago, and this time I'm afraid it is done for. Last year it was decimated, but did recover.

It is an exciting day because a critic is coming to talk with me. It makes me laugh to think that it is the first time this has happened. I have waited a long time for the professors to take notice. It is a time of suspense and stirring up in every way. Change of a radical kind is in the air. Doors open. The guardian angel has made an appearance; my days in

Nelson may be numbered, and I feel relief. It has been a long solitary pull here and time now for a fresh start. If I go, in a year or so, it will be to the sea . . . strange how those lines of Millay's have haunted me lately!

April 13th

Now THAT the snow has melted, I can see awful mole tunnels crisscrossing the front lawn in the most appalling way. But yesterday was the real first day of spring, such balmy air, such a lift! I even went out and started brushing pebbles off the lawn with an old broom (the snow ploughs shower the flower beds and grass with gravel from the drive). But with the spring languor came also a feeling of exhaustion before the work to be done outdoors, and of grief that this spring will pass and I shall hardly see X. I have done little, it sometimes seems to me, in this house but wait for people who do not or cannot come.

It did not cheer me that Carol Heilbrun, up here from Columbia yesterday, feels that what I have done best—and what she thinks altogether new in my work—is to talk about solitude. I cried bitterly last night, as if a prison door were closing. But this is a mood, of course. Solitude here is my life. I have chosen it and had better go on making as great riches as possible out of despair.

In the *Times* yesterday this by Valéry from the translation of *History and Politics*:

Under our very eyes a new society is taking shape, a wider Christendom, a *civitas mundi* less theological than medieval Christendom, less sentimental and abstract than the "humanity" of our ancestors. It is not based on the beyond but on the here and now; it draws its strength not from sentiment and opinion but from facts and necessities. Its domain is nothing but the earth; its constituents are men, races, and nations; its creative moral force is culture; its creative natural forces are place and climate; its guide is reason; its faith is the intuition of order—which is to say, the relatively modest dogma that God is not crazy.

In the spring air I decided to take Carol up to the Warners' "Farm of Contented Animals." It has been ages since I have been able to go because I am afraid of getting stuck during mud season and it is possible only rarely in winter. But for me it is always a kind of homecoming because Grace Warner, the matriarch of this great clan, has been one of my best friends in Nelson, and also because Esmeralda, the donkey I borrowed for a summer, is there and must be hugged, her soft long ears and velvety nose caressed and lumps of sugar presented to be crunched, one by one.

After the winter, the farm looked a little more frail and sunken into the earth than ever, standing in the crest of a hill, with the children's houses spread out below it near the pond, and the cow barn towering behind it. There used to be a magnificent elm beside it, but that had to be cut down last year. One looks up, wondering what is missing, what should be there in that empty space in the air.

There are always four or five cars parked around and about and I came to a stop behind them. A dog barked and barked, a cat was dozing under a wagon. For a moment we stood there getting our bearings, and then Gracie, Grace Warner's granddaughter who has kept my garden going since Perley Cole left, ran out, and Grace herself, looking a little more stooped and wan than usual, came to greet us and to be introduced to Carol.

I have brought many friends here over the years, bringing them as if to a secret treasure lost up in the hills, for there are not many such farms to be seen anywhere any longer. Gracie looks about seventeen but must be in her twenties now, a slim trim figure, her long hair loose over her shoulders, her eyes the blue eyes of her granny. Everyone in this family is crazy about animals and children, but it is Gracie who somehow finds time among all the farm chores to bring up innumerable pets and to take care of them. It was she who took us on the tour of one small shed or outbuilding after another, each like a magic box to be opened to show some dear creature.

First we went into the cow barn, the domain of Bud, Grace Warner's eldest son, who farms with his sister Helen and brings his great horses to mow my field every fall. The cows were out, but we smelled the sweet smell of ammonia and scratched the foreheads of three blunt-nosed black-and-white calves, tethered to posts. No animal at this farm is ever afraid; all are used to being handled with gentle loving care.

Then on to more magic boxes, the first a tiny shed where Carol had to go in alone as there was not room for two humans at a time . . . on the right a very old sheep and two wild-eyed goats munching on bits of hay . . . back to a row of guinea-pig cages. The next stop was at a small stable, where we pushed our way around the fat rumps of two ponies to darling Esmeralda. I had forgotten the sugar, but luckily found some large hard peppermints in the car, and these were quietly enjoyed. Esmeralda turned her great head toward me and again I was moved by those Greta Garbo eyes, the very long lashes, happy to see my old friend looking so well. Gracie told me Esmeralda's arthritis is really better and she kicks up her heels when she is let out. She is part of my private mythology of Nelson. I borrowed her as an adventure to pull me out of a bad time. She was so crippled she could hardly walk and I wanted to see whether I could cure her. It turned out to be a great success on all counts. With the help of cortisone injections and a man to clip her hoofs (donkeys are not shod; their hoofs grow like finger-nails and must be cut periodically), we got her not only walking but running away in what became a ritual caper every afternoon at four when I came to lead her out of the field to the barn for the night. By the end of the summer both Esmeralda and I had become cheerful animals again.

Grace and I talked over the winter's news while Gracie and Carol paid the silvery guinea hens and the white ducks a visit. (I heard Gracie saying that a mink had got in and killed half her ducks.) We caught up at the rabbits' winter quarters, where Carol was holding a large white rabbit in her arms. Isn't it true that long-eared animals—rabbits, donkeys— have a special charm? At any rate, Gracie's big rabbits, some with black noses and black-tipped ears, one all-black one, are beautiful creatures. We proceeded on to the bantam hens and the glorious little cock, to the muscovy ducks, and finally to the pig way down the field in his private domain. And then we came back up the hill to the horse barn, dark, piled up with hay, where at first one can just barely discern the towering rumps of the two great workhorses, Bud's pride. Gracie has two ponies in that barn now, but it is the horses that make one catch one's breath. They are huge, looming there in the dark. I never see them without marveling that man ever tamed them to his own use, for they seem like gods.

I felt that my friendship with Carol had been cemented there at the farm, something shared and enjoyed without words. And on the way home I told her more about the Warners—how hard they work, how much we all depend on them. Gracie's mother, Doris, drives one of the school buses, cleans for and takes care of three of the old ladies who are permanent residents, lifts everyone on her energy and caring, turns up if a car won't start in winter, says, "Call me at any time of the day or night if you need help." And Gracie is the hardest, swiftest worker I ever saw. It would take me a week to do what she accomplishes in a day in my garden, working with a fierce concentrated joy. She keeps in touch with my friends, those who have lived in the house when I have been away, and so, from the farm up on the hill, reaches out to Holland and San Francisco, to Wellesley and Lynnfield, pushes the boundaries of her life outward.

April 14th

JUST A BIT too much life pouring in lately, so I feel agitated and up in the air. Let me quiet down by copying a letter from Basil de Selincourt, dated December 19th, 1954, about women as poets. I looked it up as I was thinking over some things Carol said the other day.

You ask me for a personal pronouncement on women's poetry (if there is such a thing!). For several years I wanted to make an anthology of them, which several poets have now done. My hunch is that if anything is needed it is that women should quietly realize that theirs is creatively the primary role; man and his mind are an offshoot like sparks thrown out; woman is at the centre to "be still and know." One must no doubt allow that poetry and the other arts use derivative material on which the mind has worked analytically and separatively and in that degree are masculine efforts; but the whole and original and continual creative process is from within outwards, and it is the woman's prerogative to possess that place and power—a fact which she cannot fail, if she has confidence and patience, to use to effect even when handling language and other artificial modes of expression which are man-made. If women's poetry has so far shown signs of eccentricity or overemphasis, it must have been because of a feeling of strain and of a handicap to be made good. All this disappears for the woman who realizes that she is spiritually at the center. The thought and words springing from that realization and the vision natural to it are bound to have a quality which will go straight home.

Carol feels that I have willed the women in my novels to be or to fit in with Freudian views, that (like others of my generation) I have unconsciously tried to fit women into the required ethos. Even in Mélanie's case (she felt), in *The Bridge of Years*, too little was said about the business and she "gives in" to her husband, and Carol also felt that his philosophical speculations were more "real" than Mélanie's work as seen in the novel. This amazed me! Is what Carol is asking the portrait of a woman (like herself?) who has managed to bring up three children, keep her marriage very much alive and happy, and do distinguished work as a professor? Yet she told me that *three* of her married friends, women with children, have committed suicide because each felt her life was at a dead end, because she did not feel used or needed. This is a staggering figure, and gave me to think.

Later on in our conversation I asked her how she had managed. Apparently students often ask her what the price of such a life is, and she always answers, "The price is everything." But in our effete American civilization few people are willing to pay the price of anything—a garden, children, a good marriage, a work of art. And they resent the small price they manage to pay. Carol gives me the sense that she is exceptionally well-balanced, cool, discriminating, humorous, but never unfeeling. She appears to be a great exception!

Part of my agitation has been that after Carol had left I found fifty pages of manuscript I had promised to read, by a woman in her forties who is trying for a fellowship. She also paints, writes poems and short stories. She has not begun to understand what the price of excellence is. I say this with humility because I am still dashed by Carol's pointing out that certain trite phrases in my work should have been vetted. Certainly Eleanor Blair's sensitive editing eye has helped enormously in my last books. Carol admitted that *Plant Dreaming Deep* was free of these lapses.

I read the manuscript and telephoned my reactions; that at least saved writing a letter. But what I had needed was to sit down and think over the rich and fruitful day of dialogue with Carol instead of, once more, "taking in" and responding to someone else's experience. I fear that this insoluble problem of my life is becoming the leitmotif of this journal. *Basta!*

Carol would react violently against Basil's dicta, especially to the phrase that insists on a passive role for the woman, "be still and know." Where I agree with her, and was refreshed by insights I have laid aside lately, is that every artist is androgynous, that it is the masculine in a woman and the feminine in a man that proves creative. This I have always believed. But where she brought me a fresh image was to suggest that we should place all human lives in a spectrum with the very masculine man at one end and the very feminine woman at the other, and then every gradation toward the middle. I would agree also that the ultrafeminine may be as off the beam as the ultramasculine and that people of the greatest creativity and force, as well as the greatest understanding, come near the middle of the spectrum. If we could lay aside worrying about these percentages, and each of us come to a sense of moving from his *own* center (wherever it may be on the spectrum) we would obviously be a great deal freer and happier.

April 21st

LIFE COMES IN CLUSTERS, clusters of solitude, then a cluster when there is hardly time to breathe. Gracie Warner is here raking pebbles off sodden grass to try to get the lawn into shape. It is a great comfort to have her here, always cheerful and the most efficient worker I ever saw; watching her out there makes me resolve to work harder now that spring is at last in the air, or rather, "on the ground." It has been in the air for some time. Almost all the snow has gone from the flower beds, and I am gradually taking the spruce branches off. One daffodil is in bloom in front of the house, but I felt *outrage* when I left to go southward for the weekend in a thick white blizzard! And this morning it is only forty.

There is a great pelting in of life just now, but under it all runs a seam or fault that keeps me thinking. It is because of the big question Carol raised as to whether the time for passionate involvement in my life should not be past. I held back all love poems from *A Grain of Mustard Seed,* and for that reason it feels like a truncated book to me. Always before, I have wanted all facets to be included, the poems of a whole person—the conflicts, the loves, the rages, the political angst too. (I have always been beaten down for the latter, long ago by Conrad Aiken, more lately by Louise Bogan. Rhetorical poetry—and political poetry is bound to be that—is out of fashion.) But since *Plant Dreaming Deep* I feel that a false image of me is being built up, the image of a wise old party who is "above it all." I believe Carol was somewhat disappointed *not* to find that mythical person, but to find, instead, a far more vulnerable, involved, and unfinished person than she had imagined. In a letter she quoted back to me parts of the final sonnets in the "Divorce of Lovers" sequence, and the implication was that not to have given up personal life was a regression. But I think this is absurd, and shows rather *her* need of such a person than *my* need to be it. She ends, "Human beings were not meant for moderation. Yet if one needs the extremes to know the middle, as I believe with Blake and all others, perhaps moderation is the final reward of a *lived* life where we choose the center not through fear, but wisdom."

I do not think it is the business of a poet to become a

guru. It is his business to write poetry, and to do that he must remain open and vulnerable. We grow through relationships of every kind, but most of all through a relationship that takes the whole person. And it would be pompous and artificial to make an arbitrary decision to "shut the door."

The problem is to keep a balance, not to fall to pieces. In keeping her balance in her last years Louise Bogan stopped writing poems, or nearly. It was partly, I feel sure, that the detachment demanded of the critic (and especially his absorption in analyzing the work of others) is diametrically opposed to the kind of detachment demanded of the poet in relation to his own work. We are permitted to become detached only after the *shock* of an experience has been taken in, allowed to "happen" in the deepest sense. Detachment comes with examining the experience by means of writing the poem. But this is critical perception at white heat, and has nothing whatever to do with Carol's "moderation."

If I should wear the mask of that mythical person *Plant Dreaming Deep* has created in readers' minds, I would be perpetuating a myth, not growing, not casting off that skin in order to make a new one. All this is much in my mind because for the last ten days I have been contemplating a radical change in my life, one that will alarm and even rouse panic in some people who want to think of me as "the man on the hill," settled into this solitude for life.

Some days ago two friends came here, one of them Beverly Hallam, the painter, and I learned that there will be a house available for rent on an estate they have bought in Maine—a stretch of wild woodland, rocky coast, meadows running down to the sea as in Cornwall (what a dream!)—an amazing "find" along that highly populated shore line of Maine. They will build a modern house on the rocks and would rent me the "old house." I saw it yesterday, and am imagining myself into it, feeling a little clumsy. It is far grander than Nelson, but without Nelson's distinction . . . built in the 1920's, is my guess, solid and comfortable, with a superb outlook right down a golden meadow to the ocean itself. I roved about it trying to find a nest where I could work, and it is just that that I wonder about. But I have an idea that a rather sheltering paneled room on the third floor might work. And oh, the sea—"*La mer, la mer, toujours recommencée!*"

It is time for a change. My spirits are lifted by the very idea of it—living by the sea, the rhythm of the tides, the long-held dream come true. For when I was looking for a house and finally came to Nelson, I looked first at the sea. I shall have two years before the move can be made—time to feel and think my way into it. There is an already "made" garden, a lot easier to handle and better designed than mine at Nelson, the possibility of a small "greenhouse" window, a plot for a picking garden dug and ready, lots of climbing roses along a fence and clematis (even a white one), low terraces for bulbs and perennials, and an old wisteria climbing the front of the house. So the place combines a certain order and formality with the open stretch of field down to the sea.

The whole tract is almost unbelievably diverse, even to a marsh (for wild birds), a shingle beach, and big rocks. It is like a specimen tract of Maine . . . beauty and wildness.

April 28th

FROST LAST NIGHT. I felt quite sick when I looked out this morning at *white* fields, hoarfrost white. Will spring ever come?

May 6th

THERE HAS BEEN a long hiatus in this journal because I have had no days here alone, no days when time opened out before me. I find that when I have any appointment, even an afternoon one, it changes the whole quality of time. I feel overcharged. There is no space for what wells up from the subconscious; those dreams and images live in deep still water and simply submerge when the day gets scattered. But I have also experienced lately a kind of scattering: from inside, out. And since April 28th, when I wondered whether spring would ever come, we have had nothing but cold and rain, dark troubled skies, without any lightening. Yesterday, when at last we saw some blue sky, it seemed almost unbelievable. Here only the birds—the white-throated sparrows,

the dear purple finches I hear in the morning—have spoken
of spring. But slowly the grass has been greening over, and
today when I walked around the garden I counted ten or
twelve different kinds of narcissus opening at last, and the
blue periwinkles too. The garden is now all blue and yellow
for a while, the brilliant scillas and little flower that is true
Fra Angelico blue—star of the snow, maybe? There are no
leaves yet, only the slight thickening on branches and twigs.

I go out half a dozen times a day to shoot at the woodchuck. (I hope to scare him off, not to hurt him.) Already he
has eaten the first tender leaves of the hollyhocks. I have
hilarious nights because around one A.M. there is a thunder-
ous crashing on the back porch as a raccoon hurls the woodpile about to find bits of suet fallen from the bird feeder
above. She is not frightened when I put on the light. Night
before last she came to the window, laid her paws against it,
and looked at me sternly as if to say, "What do you think you
are doing here?" One night when Judy and the cats were
here this week, she got in through the cat door and dragged
out all the boxes of dry cat food standing beside it. I finally
got up and pushed a heavy barrel against the cat door; so
last night I had a good night's sleep, the first in ages, and it
certainly makes a difference in the start of a new day.

I took Judy home yesterday. She and the cats will come
up again in June for a week and she will leave the cats with
me when she goes. They are very spoiled creatures as they
have a winter and a summer home with a housekeeper
included. It was sweet, this past week, to wake with a pur-
ring presence beside me—Scrabble spent every night with
me, Fuzz Buzz upstairs with Judy. From kittenhood these
speckled sisters have led lives independent of each other,
and are jealous. If Scrabble is on my bed, Fuzz Buzz will not

come into the room, even early in the morning when she is hungry. She sits on the threshold and gives an occasional imperative mew.

My fifty-ninth birthday brought a raft of letters and flowers. I invited five friends in for champagne and sandwiches on Sunday. But on the day itself, Monday, it rained all day and I felt low in my mind. It is always really for the same reason—that so often I fail as a person, am impatient with dear Judy, whose memory fails these days. I have been helped by Jung's insights into the necessity for suffering. Sometimes I wonder whether what is often wrong with intimate human relations is not recognizing this. We fear disturbance, change, fear to bring to light and to talk about what is painful. Suffering often feels like failure, but it is actually the door into growth. And growth does not cease to be painful at any age. Jung says, "The possession of complexes does not in itself signify neurosis, for complexes are the normal foci of psychic happenings, and the fact that they are painful is no proof of pathological disturbance. Suffering is not an illness; it is the normal counterpole to happiness. A complex becomes pathological only when we think we have not got it."

It may be that when a relationship deteriorates into recriminations, it is simply that the chance for growth has been buried, "so as not to make trouble." I have learned this year more than ever before about what Jung calls "letting in the darkness," "the shadow."

> The shadow is a tight passage, a narrow door, whose painful constriction no one is spared who goes down to the deep well. But one must learn to know oneself in order to know who one is. For what comes after the door is, surprisingly enough, a boundless expanse full of

unprecedented uncertainty, with apparently no inside and no outside, no above and no below, no here and no there, no mine and no thine, no good and no bad. It is the world of water, where all life floats in suspension; where the realm of the sympathetic system, the soul of everything living, begins; where I am indivisibly this *and* that; where I experience the other in myself and the other-than-myself experiences me.

We are terribly frightened of admitting that we have been wrong, of admitting weakness; yet only when we can does the light flow in like a pardon. (Again I have gone back to that passage from Flannery O'Connor that has brought me to my knees so often after anger, in despair—the act of mercy.) I feel renewed by having gone down into Hell, the Hell of self-hatred, the Hell of war with a person whom I love, and come back to the Heaven of self-forgiveness, as well as forgiveness of the other *because* in the struggle between us, if we can face it, the truth is concealed, and could be revealed.

For weeks and months I have allowed myself to be persuaded into a frustrated pseudopeace to *spare* the other. But if there is deep love involved, there is deep responsibility toward it. We cannot afford not to fight for growth and understanding, even when it is painful, as it is bound to be. The fear of pain and of causing pain is, no doubt, a sin. At any rate, I feel back in myself again, and ready for some weeks of many interruptions, including a commencement address on May 30th.

It is a time of change and I say to myself that line from one of Rilke's "Sonnets to Orpheus," "Anticipate change as though you had left it behind you." Nelson these days becomes very luminous and real because I am slowly coming to a decision to leave it.

May 7th

AT LAST a real blue sky, but there was frost again last night!

There was no time yesterday to write of my best birthday present. Anne Woodson was to have come for lunch today, the only "free day" I shall have for some time to come. When I got back from Cambridge on Wednesday I walked into a house full of surprises—a hanging fuchsia, two marvelous rose plants, a little bag of supremely good brownies made by Nancy (aged eleven), and a note from Anne to say that she was giving me a day's time. (She had come on purpose while I was away.) This is the day she has given me and I have two poems simmering, so I had better get to work.

Gracie is out in the garden, raking leaves off the blue-bells, sowing grass seed, and if all goes well, I shall be out this afternoon myself for the first gardening this spring.

May 9th

AFTER THAT GOOD DAY, (I did write a poem and roughed out the second one) it has rained consistently and horribly. The daffodils are all beaten down *again*. But in the house I have magnificent orange parrot tulips with a very sweet scent, and white roses from my birthday; so, though my eyes are sad (looking out on the ravaged garden), my nose is very happy, smelling these sweet smells.

My capacity for weeping is really becoming a grotesque affliction. What is the drug that stops tears? This morning I have written a few "real" letters, real as opposed to dutiful, and that always helps to tell me where I am. It is a bleak plateau at the moment in the inner world. But we need only to come to terms with reality to have some foundation on which to stand firm. When I got up, every breath I drew came out of pain, mental anguish, so acute for a time that I was immobilized by it, trying to breathe. Finally I put clean sheets on the bed, fed the birds, Punch too of course, and the greedy marmalade twins who come and glare at me through the kitchen windows. I do long for a lovable (they are not) and loving animal. It will be splendid when the pussies come back for the summer!

I feel a bit firmer now. It always comes back to the same necessity: go deep enough and there is a bedrock of truth, however hard. It looks as if I were "meant" to be alone, and that any hope of happiness is *not* meant. Am I too old to acquire the knack for happiness? Too old, perhaps, ever to take in another's life to share with mine on a permanent basis? If so, I must make do with what I have . . . and what I have is a great richness of friends and a positively ardent love of nature. Not nothing!

May 15th

It is *the* moment now. Daffodils, many different kinds, are glorious, in spite of a whole day of hard rain and wind. Small bright red tulips wonderful also. It is *the* moment because the leaves on the trees have not yet sprung, so the light and blue sky shine through feathery, just-swelling twigs. The structure is still visible and that is what gives the effect of stained glass. I saw a hummingbird yesterday. Both purple and gold finches swarm around the feeder, and I have heard an oriole, though have not yet caught a glimpse of him, devouring the maple flowers high up in the air. Yesterday Gracie cut grass for the first time. I have put in six rosebushes, these last days, and about two hundred small things, such as petunias, columbine, lupines, to fill out borders decimated by this cruel winter. I fear the azaleas have been blighted by the two hard frosts we have suffered since May 1st.

I resent having to run around in this best of all months here except October. But so it is. I am just back from two days in Richmond, Virginia, at that Miller and Rhoads "do" for writers. I get absurdly nervous about clothes; the whole society atmosphere throws me . . . I shall never, never feel at home in it. It all went off well, yet I came home full of misgivings and disgruntlement. Why is it so upsetting to be involved with the *selling* of books? How does a writer of my kind survive the big machine? And to be a witness, even for a short time, of the way in which it works creates panic.

This time the saving grace was instant friendship with two of the writers. One, C.D.B. Bryan, had for me all the charm of the young Englishmen I used to see in London, elegant and fair, open and humorous, the sharp edges refined. The other was Thomas Fleming, Irish, exuberant, tough, sensitive. They were a breath of fresh air.

But, as Ted Weeks reminded me as we parted, one gets the reaction from so much "exposure" two days later, and I have been dead tired these last two days.

May 16th

A GRAY DAY ... but, strangely enough, a gray day makes the
bunches of daffodils in the house have a particular radiance,
a kind of white light. From my bed this morning I could look
through at a bunch in the big room, in that old Dutch blue-
and-white drug jar, and they glowed. I went out before
seven in my pajamas, because it looked like rain, and picked
a sampler of twenty-five different varieties. It was worth getting up early, because the first thing I saw was a scarlet tana-
ger a few feet away on a lilac bush—stupendous sight! There
is no scarlet so vivid, no black so black.

May 20th

WE ARE HAVING a heat wave—ninety yesterday afternoon. It
is hard because the daffodils, so crisp and fresh a day ago,
are burning up and fading. For a brief moment now the
garden is rather wonderful. In another two or three days the
leaves on the trees will be out and the transparent veil will
thicken into a curtain. I shall not be able to see the hills
below the house again till autumn. When the trees are still in

flower is the best time for seeing birds. The oriole gives his
sharp single note every few minutes, up in the maples eating
the flowers. I have seen him but always against the sun, so I
have not yet got that flash of red-gold on the wings. Last
evening I went out on the porch and sat for half an hour,
entranced by the delicate color, the soft reds and pale greens
of trees at the foot of the meadow . . . swallows flying in and
out of the barn . . . a song sparrow singing an evening song in
the locust.

It looks as if Nevada, the single white rose beside the
barn that had grown to nearly eight feet in height and was
covered with flowers in late May, has died.

The treasures in the garden now are all tiny—blue wood
anemones in a small carpet round the viburnum are a great
success; the fritillaries with their strange chequered bells
have done well under the forsythia; leucojum, those large
white bells, each with a tiny green spot drawn on the petals
(like a child's drawing of an imaginary flower) are thriving;
the white violets with a fine blue stripe at the throat are out
too—and I am furious to have to be away these days. The
changes come so fast. I want to be *here*.

May 25th

THE SEASON is as changeable, fitful, and maddening as I am
myself these days that are choked with too many demands
and engagements. It is really a long time since I had what I
think of as my "real" life. Since I wrote five days ago the

temperature went down to twenty, but somehow most things have survived. I wrapped the clematis, so very tender now, in burlap bags one night.

The blast of cold was followed by days of high wind and sun, a dazzling air as light dappled through leaves, all in motion. Now we have Scotch mist, and it looks like rain, badly needed. Yesterday I managed to sow all the annuals, and to put in boxes of nicotiana, parsley, some columbine, and more pansies, fighting blackflies that swarmed around my face the whole time. It was a relief to get it done, the worst spring job. Now for a while I can enjoy the garden as the great spring sequence proceeds. The daffodils are nearly over, but tulips and bleeding heart have opened.

It is a catastrophe to have five baby woodchucks under the barn, though they are adorable, like small toy bears. Of course, they have eaten down the hollyhocks. But I take these disasters more philosophically than I used to. I am learning not to take it all too personally, I guess, and not to mind failure. The garden is growth and change and that means loss as well as constant new treasures to make up for a few disasters. The blue pansies are wonderful this year. Blue is the most exciting color in the garden, I think. And these blues are everywhere now: Virginia bluebells, grape hyacinths, blue primroses, and wood anemones. Soon there will be bluebells in the little wood and wild phlox here and there.

Anne Woodson is coming for lunch, and it is lovely to think how attentively she will look at it all.

I have longed for one person with whom everything could be shared, but I am slowly making my peace with the knowledge that this will never happen. It would be good to root the intensity somewhere for good, but I guess it will have to be rooted in the work. Perhaps I feel dispersed this

month because I am not at the moment engaged in a com-
manding work, a work that would force me to lay aside small
commitments and demands and get on with it, come Hell or
high water.

May 28th

SOMETIMES WONDERFUL PRESENTS arrive from nowhere. Yesterday an unknown sent me, out of the blue, a book called
Loneliness, by Clark E. Moustakas. I opened to this passage:
"I began to see that loneliness is neither good nor bad, but a
point of intense and timeless awareness of the Self, a beginning which initiates totally new sensitivities and aware-
nesses, and which results in bringing a person deeply in
touch with his own existence and in touch with others in a
fundamental sense."

I am leading a cluttered life these days. The baby woodchucks are devouring the garden, but they are so happy—
how can I kill them? The raccoon wakes me every night at
about one A.M. with a shattering noise of logs being tossed
about on the kitchen porch. When I put on the light the raccoon looks up at me with cold curiosity and slowly heaves
herself up the pole onto the roof. But she comes down again
in a few minutes and it all starts again. Last night I gave up
and let her have her way. The three barn cats come and yowl
at me five times a day and I weakly give in and feed them. I
dislike the two orange males, but the tabby I have cared for
all winter and truly love—and she is so pregnant!

En plus, Punch has a huge swelling over his left eye, and I fear may be going blind. After the next two speeches are over (one a commencement address at New England College on Sunday), I must get him to a vet. He doesn't scream any more, poor dear. Birds are so brave! I remember D. H. Lawrence's poem in which he says they are "never sorry for themselves." Punch talks to me in his intimate voice still, but his joyful morning scream is no more.

I am badgered by all these anxieties, but they are not what I mean by *clutter*. Clutter is what silts up exactly like silt in a flowing stream when the current, the free flow of the mind, is held up by an obstruction. I spent four hours in Keene yesterday getting the car inspected and two new tires put on, also finding a few summer blouses. The mail has accumulated in a fearful way, so I have a huge disorderly pile of stuff to be answered on my desk. In the end what kills is not agony (for agony at least asks something of the soul) but everyday life.

The immense value of a love affair is, of course, that it burns up the clutter like the trash it is. When X and I first met life was nothing but a long hymn of praise. I am revising those poems now, so I am very much aware of the difference between those first weeks after X came into my life and where our relationship is now. What is asked of us now is to be tolerant, patient, to try to bridge the gaps between our personalities and temperaments, even between our values . . . and the *Gestalt* of our lives. When X leaves the job for a week, the job can be cut out entirely. But my job can never be cut out. That would mean an end to feeling and its analysis, an end to perception, and all that becomes not less acute for me when X and I are together. How well said by James Kirkup in his poem "The Poet":

Each instant of his life, a task, he never rests,
And works most when he appears to be doing nothing.
The least of it is putting down in words
What usually remains unwritten and unspoken,
And would so often be much better left
Unsaid, for it is really the unspeakable
That he must try to give an ordinary tongue to.

And if, by art and accident,
He utters the unutterable, then
It must appear as natural as a breath,
Yet be an inspiration. And he must go,
The lonelier for his unwanted miracle,
His singular way, a gentle lunatic at large
In the societies of cross and reasonable men.

I feel cluttered when there is no time to analyze experience. That is the silt—unexplored experience that literally chokes the mind. Too much comes into this house—books I am asked to read and comment on, manuscripts, letters, an old friend who wants my opinion about a journal (whether it is publishable), and so on. *This* is the clutter, not woodchuck or raccoon!

June 4th

AT LAST I'm off the roller coaster, the last public appearance over for a while. Today for the first time in ages I put my work first before writing a single letter, and am writing poems.

But I must speak now of one piece of mail that told me that Emerson Crocker had died of a tumor of the brain. I mourn him as a man of rare kindness, especially toward the old. And he was kind in imaginative ways like appearing at dear old Ethel's door with milkshakes, and sandwiches, and then sitting down for an hour to have lunch with her and a good talk—a truly *gentle* man. How little he can be spared in an age in which gentleness is becoming the rarest of qualities! Against this I put the ugly fact that a friend's suitcase was stolen as she stood in line to buy a ticket in Penn Station on her way to her fiftieth class reunion. And against Emerson's gentleness I place the atmosphere at Queens University (where I read poems day before yesterday); there not only must every office door be locked at all times, but every drawer of every desk and every file. No valuable book can be left out, unprotected, on a shelf! So the atmosphere is that of a prison. How be aware of the human compact as viable when an old woman is robbed in a public place and when an institution of learning, so rich in gifts to its students, must arm itself against them?

I place Emerson's gentleness and reverence for life against what I hear of the young historians of science busily putting George Sarton down. Of course he had weaknesses, perhaps stemming from the fact that he was a man of the nineteenth century, not the twentieth; thus he never understood Freud. He was not a sociologist in the modern sense, either. He was really a historian of the old-fashioned school but dealt with elements in history that had been overlooked or written about piecemeal. Surely his greatness came from a unifying vision that places art, science, and religion as the great inventions of man and thus, as he so often said, moves toward "the humanizing of science" through examining its history. He liked to emphasize not only the international character of experimental science, but also that every break-through rested on the work of many anonymous and devoted men and that the final "genius" stood on their shoulders. So the young historians of science stand on George Sarton's shoulders; but of course he is the father-figure, who must be beaten down, and only when he has become the grandfather of the history of science will he, perhaps, come into his own.

> Come let us mock at the great
> That had such burdens on the mind
> And toiled so hard and late
> To leave some monument behind,
> Nor thought of the levelling wind.
>
> Come let us mock at the wise;
> With all those calendars whereon
> They fixed old aching eyes,
> They never saw how seasons run,
> And now but gape at the sun.
>
> . . . .
>
> Mock mockers after that
> That would not lift a hand maybe
> To help good, wise or great
> To bar that foul storm out, for we
> Traffic in mockery.

So Yeats has the last word.

June 12th

WHAT AN EXTRAORDINARY spring that brings us frost in June!
The temp went down to thirty-two in the last two days, but
the cool, clear days are a blessing. It means the lilacs have
stayed in flower for two weeks; they are just beginning to
pale off now. The lavender ones turn first to a kind of silver,
then sad brown; and the marvelous deep purple ones become
lavender as they go. Have I ever had tulips in bloom as late
as this? There are still three bright red ones with white lilac
in a jar in the big room. And as I looked at them this morning I thought that a clear bright red is almost as rare in the
garden as a clear bright blue. The peony red turns toward
purple, alas.

I am devoted to raccoons, but I am quite cross with the
one who comes every night and hurls the woodpile apart,
then an hour later bangs the ash cans around. I now have to
keep the cat door closed against him . . . as well as against
the homeless cats. There are now three of these cats, and
there is much glaring and hissing as various factions meet. I
feed them all, dashing out with dishes to hide under bushes
so my own jealous cats will not be upset; so it is rather like a
Howdy-Doody for cats here, with a waitress who serves cus-
tomers outside!

It is good to be back on a schedule. Norton will publish a
new book of poems to celebrate my sixtieth birthday next

spring. I must have the manuscript in their hands by the end of September. As soon as I have a deadline, I work much better. Time unbounded is hard to handle.

June 15th

THE WHITE TREE PEONY has opened. How did it survive the tons of snow the ploughs piled over it, to present to me now with a single immense miracle of a flower? I keep going out to look at it, as I am revising a poem that uses the white peony as an image. Of course, the problem with revising is that it is done cold, with diminished critical intensity. Inspiration is criticism at white heat. This morning I nearly despaired.

The difficulty is rendering the combination of crispness, yet of flowing, as light and shadows play on the petals. The design is very distinct always, not at all *flou*, but the effect is of flowing, never rigid like the iris.

I hate to leave the garden for Maine during the supreme week of the year when iris and peonies are out, but I am surely at the thin edge of exhaustion these days. It is bad when one gets to the state where even joy becomes too costly, when really only dark and sleep are welcome. This morning I stayed in bed till after nine and actually slept for ten hours. (I took the ash cans indoors and, except for a wrangle between raccoon and cat, the night was quiet for once.) How does one rest? I am trying to do it by not hurrying, by not allowing the pressure to build. One step at a time. It is like climbing out of a deep well.

June 21st

BACK FROM a weekend away with X. I knew when I left Friday afternoon that the moment of glory was about to come, but I had not expected quite the explosion I found in the dusk when I got back just before nine. Most of the peonies, the classic swanlike ones with a scarlet thread through their centers, are open, and most of the double pinks as well (my least favorite). Iris is open everywhere, the huge red poppies, the beauty bush, and a bright pink single rose way down at the end of the big border. Everything is dry as a bone. I got up at six to water, and to pick flowers for the house.

But it was not a quiet night, for at about eleven the raccoon began banging around outside, although I had brought the ash cans indoors again. But this persistent and clever beastie is *determined* to get in through the cat door and steal boxes of cat food. What a hilarious night it turned out to be! I piled wood on a chair outside on the porch, and jammed the chair in such a way that it seemed impossible to budge. Not at all! Half an hour later I heard a crash and when I got there and turned on the porch light, I found the raccoon busily pushing at a twenty-pound can of birdseed, the final bastion against the cat door. I shouted at her, got a dirty look, and went back to bed. This was repeated about five times. Each time I added more weight—all to no avail. Finally I took the rifle and shot to scare her off, but she came back very shortly. Then I went out three times barefoot, unwound the hose, and wet her with a thin hard jet, where she sat on the porch roof.

By two I was dead tired and must have fallen asleep, after banking heavy things both outside and inside the cat door. But when I got up this morning the raccoon had won! Everything was thrown about and several boxes of cat food, dragged outside through the cat door, were left on the porch, spilled open and hardly touched. I guess it is malice and impishness rather than hunger that keeps this game going! The only answer is to close up the cat door for good, with nails and a piece of board.

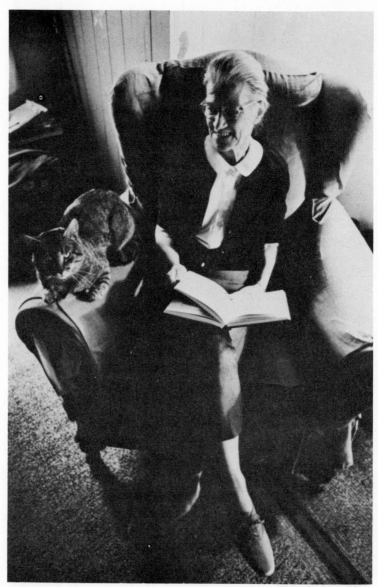

Photo by Mort Mace

June 23rd

ALMOST TOO MUCH happens these days. How can I be enough aware of all that opens and dies so quickly in the garden? It takes a whole year of work and waiting for this supreme moment of the great snow-white peonies—and then they are gone! I was thinking about it as I lay in bed this morning, and also of Mildred's wise remark, "The roots of love need watering or it dies." When she leaves, the house is at peace. Beauty and order have returned, and always she has left behind a drop of balm, such as that phrase; so her work here is a work of art. There is a mystical rite under the material act of cleaning and tidying, for what is done with love is always more than itself and partakes of the celestial orders.

It does not astonish or make us angry that it takes a whole year to bring into the house three great white peonies and two pale blue iris. It seems altogether right and appropriate that these glories are earned with long patience and faith (how many times this late spring I have feared the lilacs had been frost-killed, but in the end they were as glorious as ever before), and also that it is altogether right and appropriate that they cannot last. Yet in our human relations we are outraged when the supreme moments, the moments of flowering, must be waited for . . . and then cannot *last*. We reach a summit, and then have to go down again.

Maybe patience is the last thing we learn. I remember
Jean Dominique, old and blind, saying to me, *"On attend
toujours."* I was under thirty then and she was over sixty and
I was amazed to think that someone so old could still wait
for someone so intensely. But now I know that one does so
all one's life.

July 7th

BACK FROM Greenings Island, my annual pilgrimage with
Judy to visit Anne Thorp. The island, three miles long, faces
the mountains of Mt. Desert and stands just at the mouth of
Somes Sound opposite Southwest Harbor—an island of tall fir
and spruce, of many-colored soft mosses, blueberry patches,
and a long open meadow that rolls down to a salt-water pool.
We come here to a timeless world, steeped in tradition,
where for a week or so we are sheltered by the safety and
comfort of the Victorian era when the many-roomed, shin-
gled ark of a house was built by Anne's father, in the 1890's.
We come back to all the familiar joys—sitting on our balcony
to watch the silent sails glide past up the Sound and the
ever-changing clouds and light and shadow on the water and
on the hills, gathering mussels or blueberries for supper,
making bunches of wildflowers, finding tiny trees and cush-
ions of moss for Japanese gardens to be created when we are
home again, going to bed with a candle up the great staircase (there is no electricity), sinking into our twin brass

beds and talking for hours side by side before we fall asleep. We become children again, assigned small domestic tasks, joining "the family" for meals at the big table on the porch downstairs where Anne says grace, queen of this large yet intimate kingdom, and where we may sit for an hour after supper discussing anything and everything, exchanging the news of a year, turning from politics to philosophy as the sun sets and it is finally time to go in to the fire.

The days here are timeless partly because they are both orderly and free. We lead our own lives, yet without any of the usual stresses and demands. I work in the morning in what was Dardy's room (Dardy, the Thorps' nurse, long since dead), next to the nursery. At noon Judy and I walk through the woods, punctuated by bird song, and out across the field, among black-eyed Susans, patches of heather, and an occasional clump of the delicate lavender harebells, for a swim in the pool. In the evenings we read aloud. Many of my books have been first heard here in manuscript in the cavernous "big room" before a log fire, someone lying on the bear rug, Anne on the sofa, and other guests scattered about beyond the bright ring of light shed by the Aladdin lamp. This is a far more rewarding way of "publishing" a work than when it finally comes to Nelson in bound and printed copies six months later.

Since my parents' death this island has become the one unchangeable place in my life and Anne Thorp the nearest thing to family except Judy. It is the place of renewal and of safety, where for a little while there will be no harm or attack and, while every sense is nourished, the soul rests.

Someday I hope to write at length about the island, but today I want to define the particular quality of the person who inhabits it like some life-giving Ceres—to celebrate

Anne Thorp herself. During this past year I have been thinking a lot about the lives of women, their problems and conflicts, and of the values that an unmarried woman may occasionally represent. Anne is a good example of those values.
For her, life itself has been the creation, but not in the usual
mode as wife, mother, and grandmother. Had Anne married,
she would have led a different life and no doubt a rich one,
but she would not have been able to give what she does here
and in the way she does. There are several houses involved,
all to be filled with family or friends who come and go
throughout the summer. Anne's life has reached out in many
directions, not only through the Shady Hill School (where
she was my teacher in the seventh grade), but before that to
France after World War I to care for refugee children in a
Franco-American orphanage, and after World War II to Ger-
many to work with the Unitarian Service Committee in help-
ing to found a Neighborhood House in Bremen. So the island
gathers to itself a rich variety of people of all ages and races.

Down in the boathouse there is sure to be some little boy
absorbed in making a boat from driftwood, and off in the
woods an old lady botanizing or birding, while a pair of
young lovers sit on a rocky point having a long probing talk
about their future, and a whole family is off fishing in one of
the work boats. And, through it all, a knapsack slung over
her shoulder, Anne moves with a light step, getting a house
ready for new guests, taking a child by the hand to show him
the fish hawk's nest, or asking Judy and me, "What about a
cup of tea?" When she goes off island, as she may once or
twice a summer, there is a perceptible vacuum . . . something
is missing. Someone is not there who holds all the threads
together in her hands. We are faintly alarmed, a little lonely.

Now in her seventies, Anne is stooped, but her profile is

still that of Nefertiti and her long stride that of a goddess. Goddess? The word springs to mind because (can it be fifty years ago?) as a child I watched her dancing the folk dance called "Goddesses" in the Longfellow House garden, and there has been an association ever since. A granddaughter of Longfellow, she has seemed to me, a European, the personification of the American aristocrat. This implies a deeply felt *noblesse oblige*, the very opposite of "privilege" in the sense of demanding recognition or being exempted in any way from ordinary human endeavor and responsibility. Here is a personal largess, a largess of giving to life in every possible way, that makes her presence itself a present. She would not be angry with a mouse. She would not give money without giving herself as she did for many years at the Shady Hill School. And all that may be an inherited grace, but Anne, within yet apart from her family, is unique. Of what is her genius made? That is the mystery I have been contemplating this morning.

Perhaps the key is in her capacity to make herself available on any day, at any time, to whatever human joy or grief longs to be fulfilled or assuaged by sharing . . . longs to pour itself out and to be understood. So a teddy bear will materialize as if by magic for a one-year-old who has stubbed a toe; so a young woman who cannot decide whom to marry can have a long talk in perfect peace; so a very old lady can discuss with gusto the coming presidential election and feel a fire to match her own rise up in Anne's blue eyes. The participation is never passive, shot through with a sudden gust of laughter as it often is, always vivid and original. For me, who am always split between art and life, the wonder is that Anne's immense capacity for experience seems never to be strained or burdened by the many threads she holds in her hands, especially on the island. This is the heart of the mystery. How does she do it? How does she isolate the moment, the human moment, from all the rest? Perhaps because in this she is a poet. I do not think of what I should be doing in the garden or of an unanswered letter when I am writing a poem. I am all there in the timeless world of creation. Anne lives each moment of the day as if it were the first and the last, with the whole of herself.

When Judy and I evoke the joys of Greenings Island—perhaps at Christmastime when we are sitting by the fire at Nelson—we come back to a few precise images. One goes back to the year when great horned owls nested on the island and Anne imitated for us the mating cry. Her arms became wings. She herself *was* an owl and the sounds that owl produced were memorable and can still reduce us, now, many years later to tears of laughter. Another image is of a day when we had walked over to another house where there were children. Anne wore her long red cape, shade of the days when she was a student at Vassar, and, suddenly inspired, spread it out around her in batlike wings and swooped about to the delight of the children, perhaps a little frightened by the authenticity of this newborn witch in their garden. What I keep in my heart is catching Anne as I came down the wide staircase at the end of a morning's work, sitting in the "office" in her father's chair at the big roll-top desk, her head bent over accounts or a letter, a little remote, absorbed in the dispatch box, and, suddenly amused, smiling a secret smile. From this last visit, there is a fresh image of Anne, standing with us on the rocky shore at precisely ten minutes after eight in the evening to wait in high expectancy for the immense, deep orange moon to slip up over Sutton's Island and then swing into the sky, shedding a perfectly straight unbroken path over the still waters.

I have not captured the secret—who ever will?—but how lovely to have dipped for an hour into the mystery of this dearest of friends before Nelson crowds in again!

Nelson greeted me with an explosion of roses *and* Japanese beetles, the garden terribly dry after more than a month of little or no rain. I also discovered an indefinite number of kittens under the porch. The little wild tabby evidently feels safe there; she is terribly thin and being pursued again by her horrible randy sons, one of them no doubt the father of these kittens.

I got up at six and watered, then restored myself and the house to our old communion by arranging two glorious bunches of flowers, a celebration of summer. Here on the mantel it is foxglove, honeysuckle, a huge Peace rose, a white Martagon lily, some branches of the small white clematis, and a branch of that bright pink single rose that flowers only once in a season. Outside in the garden Souvenir de la Malmaison and Deuil de Paul Fontaine are in flower, one pale pink, the other very dark red, old-fashioned cushion-shaped roses as lovely for their names as for their presences.

It is hard to get to work indoors when there is so much waiting to be attended to outside. But I must, as I have only five days here before I go off again for a week with X. It is a checkerboard summer, but I try to take it philosophically, step by step, and joy by joy.

After watering, I went back to bed for breakfast and read a cogent essay on Thoreau in the Sunday *Times*. The author feels that the renaissance of Thoreau is unrealistic because his cultivation of the "eternal moment" precluded human relations and thus he is not a reliable guru for our times— times when "social man" is having to grow painfully and we are asked to take in more and more. To a great extent Thoreau wished to be and succeeded in being an island apart from the main. We are going to have to outgrow the myth that this is either possible or good. One reason I felt impelled to keep this journal for a year was because I think that *Plant Dreaming Deep* has created the myth of a false Paradise. I want to destroy that myth. In fact, I see my function as quietly destroying myths, even those of my own making, in order to come closer and closer to reality and to accepting reality. Although Mrs. Stevens herself is a romantic in her way of life (as all worshipers of the White Goddess are), she is not romantic in her view of it.

In my lifetime I have seen one comforting myth after another taken apart as I, like everyone else, have tried to come to grips with hard truth. We have had to accept civilized man as the most cruel of all animals, to recognize that, given absolute power, we all become sadists (the German camps, Lieutenant Calley, et cetera), that wickedness is not a religious concept useful to terrify people into submission but an absolute reality, that each of us battles within the self. We have had to accept that democracy in the United States has been imperceptibly taken over and transformed into government by cartels and power groups, including organized labor and the military, and has almost eluded the grasp of "the people"; so we are engaged in a dreadful war in which no one can believe and which we seem helpless to end. We have come to understand that blacks, far from being "liberated," are still oppressed in every possible way. And now we are increasingly aware that women must fight a difficult and painful war for their autonomy and wholeness. We have had to swallow the hard truth that boys and girls of even the middle class are delinquent in large numbers, take to drugs because something is so lacking in the ethos we have created that they look for "illumination" from this most troubling of sources. We have seen our public schools physically destroyed by the students out of rage and hunger. And, hardest of all, we have had to admit that Simone Weil is probably right when she says that to relieve God of responsibility for the horrors of the world as it is, we have to put Him at an infinite distance.

The marvel is that there are still so many people of courage who go on fighting in spite of all these reasons for despair.

The night before I left for Maine I saw five minutes on CBS (Charles Kurault on the road) that left me in tears. It told the story of a black man, Mr. Black, a bricklayer from North Carolina in his ninety-third year, a thin eager face. Mr. Black was flown, at government expense, to an African country in dire need of building materials and the *expertise* to learn how to use their own earth for bricks. He showed them how to dig clay, how to make the forms, how to build whole villages at little or no expense. What an imaginative act, for once, on the part of the powers that be! And how marvelous for him, a very old man, to see his gift used, to discover what he had to share! I took it as a parable, and that is why I wept.

July 8th

BILL BROWN was to have come for lunch. He has lost both his parents in this last month, his dear father from a heart attack just the other day. I have been thinking of him so much, an orphan now like me. Orphan at fifty? The word

sprang from my remembering a letter I had from Harry
Greene, then in his eighties, when my father died. It began,
"Now you are an orphan too." Just now Bill phoned to say he
was ill and could not come, after all.

At the end of our talk his aunt, Amy Loomis, now ninety,
asked to speak to me. It is characteristic that in the midst of
her loss what she wanted to tell me about was a vivid
memory she keeps of my mother picking flowers at Mrs.
Merriman's in Intervale, of the flowers in her hands (there
was marvelous salpiglossis, I remember) and the way she
held them. Mrs. Merriman's garden was on one side of a
sloping velvety lawn, shaped like a maple leaf, with many
small beds of annuals and perennials. How my mother
enjoyed picking flowers early in the morning, and arranging
them—flowers from a garden someone else weeded!

Our yearly visit to Intervale was a great blessing, very
much to my father and mother what Greenings Island has
become for me. The house was spacious, formal, and full of
treasures, among them a cabinet of rare shells, kept locked.
Every afternoon at precisely four the chauffeur in the black
Pierce Arrow came to take us for a short drive to a lake, wa-
terfall, or "view." At half past four Mrs. Merriman took a
small pillbox from her purse and offered me from it a single
malted milk tablet as a special treat. One summer I spent
happy hours making a tiny anthology of poems for her
pocket, illustrated with watercolors of flowers. Sometimes I
long to spend the rest of my life doing just that—making
things for people I love—and never to publish again.

The *New Statesman* for July 2nd has a review of LM's
book about Katherine Mansfield. At last, at eighty-three, LM
has told her story. Until now we have had only the bowdler-
ized version of it that appears in the Mansfield journals.

Murry was not anxious to have the truth known, of course. But even at the time the journals were published (edited by him) it seemed unnecessarily cruel to leave in the excruciating bit about the slow way LM ate bananas. Kot always used to say that she was a "good person," one of the very few people of whom he wholly approved.

The review by Claire Tomlin is headed "The Wife's Story." The last part reads:

> This pendulum swinging between the elusive Murry who could not look after Katherine and the utterly devoted LM continued to last to the last few weeks of Katherine's life, when she withdrew from both. Until then, the situation was this: Murry was quite incapable of nursing Katherine, making practical arrangements for her comfort—she was usually in pain and always weak—or even of loving her enough. LM alone would nurse and love and dust and light fires and shop and sew on buttons and bring the breakfast tray and the lunch tray and run after her with jackets that Katherine childishly flung down. There is no doubt that she, with her genius and her illness, needed "a wife" as well as a husband. And LM was that wife as truly as Murry was her husband; a wife whose protective instincts often maddened K into rage, but to whom she wrote in 1922: "try and believe and keep on believing without signs from me that I do love you and want you for my wife." Without her Katherine Mansfield would not have been able to write even what she did. Koteliansky called LM Katherine's "sole and only friend"; in a sense she allowed Katherine to live the two lives—though both were brief—that a woman who burns with a desire to work and to love needs. In allowing us to trace the course of this extraordinary friendship from adolescent

enthusiasm through many trials and quarrels to the final mutual acceptance, Miss Baker has continued her service to her friend.

Of course, the big question is why the word "wife" rather than the word "mother." What LM did was, in fact, to "mother" but out of a different-from-motherly kind of love, and certainly Katherine's feelings for her were ambivalent. The point Kot always made was that LM, often behaving like a slave and treated like one, never became one. She kept her dignity, her wholeness, and her love intact—no small feat.

Perhaps the truth is that Murry needed a mother. He was constitutionally unable to be the nurse that KM needed, and their marriage began to break apart as soon as she needed a nurse and could not play the role of mother any longer. So within the trio all the roles shifted. Murry became the lover, summoned when KM felt well enough to have a lover, and LM became the wife of the creator in Katherine who needed one. Professional women do need wives and many have joked about this fact. And we have seen instances of homosexual relationships where it seemed to work: Gertrude Stein and Alice B. Toklas come to mind. But the woman wife of a professional woman has to be extraordinarily selfless and still have a strong ego to keep her dignity—and Toklas really came into her own as a personality only after Gertrude Stein's death.

July 10th

YESTERDAY I felt so tired that I accomplished nothing whatever. It was a hot humid day, clouding over, that waiting-for-rain tension. But the clouds blew away finally and I had to water the garden after all. Things are terribly dry; yet the garden flourishes and is quite glorious again, for the great blue spires of delphinium are in flower, also white Madonna lilies, and here and there a Japanese iris, luminous pale blue or violet. The round bed for these Japanese iris near the barn is where I also scattered seed from the strange bluish-red fringed poppies I brought from Greenings Island. ALT thinks they were brought there in the beak of a bird. It is the first time I have managed to get them to take hold here—an exciting event, for I have never seen this flower anywhere before except on the island. The roses tumble about in opulent clouds these days.

At the time, in a doldrum, one is unaware of what a blank day like yesterday can do to replenish energy. First the total letdown like a fountain gone dry, and then the sudden rush of energy the next day. Today I feel centered, powerful, happy, and have not only written some letters long on my mind, but also read over all the poems for the new book. It really will work, I think, and especially as a total contrast to *Mustard Seed*. This is a flowery book, full of images of flowers and of trees and light and shadow on flowers and leaves, mostly love poems.

Certain days gather to themselves tensions of a superficial kind. Yesterday was a day when no machine would work. I had car trouble; then (the last straw!) when I turned on the TV for news it wouldn't work. It is thirteen years old and has served me well. I dashed down to Keene on an impulse and bought a new one. When I turned it on, I got the memorial tribute to Louis Armstrong. I wouldn't have missed the St. Louis Blues sung out on that trumpet for anything. Something shone from that man, a rare thing, real *joy*. It is becoming exceedingly rare among artists of any kind. And I have an idea that those who can and do communicate it are always people who have had a hard time. Then the joy has no smugness or self-righteousness in it, is inclusive not exclusive, and comes close to prayer.

July 26th

TWO WEEKS since my last entry. I get a few days off and then there are guests or I am away. The drought goes on, but the garden flourishes, especially when I manage to get up at six and water for an hour. That makes all the difference to the shallow-rooted annuals. It is now the hour of the shirley poppies—every morning I go out to pick the dozen or more fresh ones that have opened, white, pink, red in every variation, their diaphanous petals among the loveliest things I ever see, the fallen petals silken to the touch. Their delicacy is delightful at this season when most flowers are opaque and the garden becomes a jungle. There are lilies opening also. I have a huge pink one on the mantel here with some pale pink phlox and big blue thistles. Down in the border below the kitchen woodchucks have again eaten all the phlox and all the asters.

I got back from a week by the sea with X, absolutely starved for trees, for shade, for the distinction of Nelson, and sick of the affluent society as one sees it in every real "shore place" these days—sadly changed since X bought the house there. It reminded me of Knocke—the chiaroscuro skies over salt marshes, the dunes and wide sandy beach, the umbrellas, and the immemorial games of children making sand castles, bringing up pails of water from the sea to damp walls down, and (something I had forgotten) burying each other in the sand. This is quite a dreadful image, only the child's head left out and his body unable to move under the heavy weight.

It was a real holiday on one level, but on the deep level a rather troubling and frustrating time. This journal began in September nearly a year ago and has recorded, whatever I may have wished not to speak of, a steady decline in my relationship with X.

August 3rd

MY MOTHER'S BIRTHDAY. It is strange that I have not been able to write about her, or so very little. When I have tried, the anguish got in the way and I fail to remember or to be able to communicate her vivid grace, her laughter (we used to laugh together till tears rolled down our cheeks), into her seventies her swift impassioned walk, as though she were on her way to a momentous destination although she may have been only en route to buy fish for dinner. She savored life more than anyone I have ever known. It could be seen in the way she looked at everything with that quizzical, observant, total attention—a flower, a Chinese jar, our beautiful silver cat, Cloudy, or George Sarton when they sat opposite each other for a ritual cup of tea in the garden. People turned to her as to a warm light, warm and clear, never sentimental. She was politically radical, outspoken, quick to anger or elation, and extremely brave. Almost everyone who ever met my mother even once remembers her vividly, as if it had been a memorable event. Eleanor Blair has often reminded me of their first meeting, when Mother ran down the stairs to greet her with a bunch of flowers, for I had told her it was Eleanor's birthday. And even people who did not know her personally often folded away and kept forever the charming embroidered dresses she designed for Belgart: the brilliant colors, emerald green, orange, pinks, reds, blues, still glow. In just the same way her letters were kept . . . how many little bundles have come to me in these last years after her death!

All this is the brilliant, life-enhancing side of a woman who battled ill-health all her life and was twice transplanted radically, first from England to Belgium when she married my father, and then from Belgium to America when we came here as refugees in 1916. In spite of her genius for friendship, the tragedy of my mother was that after the second transplanting some deep reserve kept her from making close friends again. She had to go back to Europe to drink from the deep wells. Anne Thorp is the one exception. So the long letters that went back and forth to and from Belgium, Switzerland, and France were really a lifeline. My mother remained an exile in America.

She was extravagant by nature, extravagant in giving, but held to a tight rein of near poverty till the very last years. My father was a typical bourgeois Belgian about money matters—for years my mother did not know what he earned. He doled out a monthly allowance that was never quite enough, and would not discuss money matters with her. So it was she who earned by teaching, by designing for Belgart, what sent me to camp and through school and what made the "little extra" she needed to help support a White Russian family in Florence who had come to her attention by chance—and a thousand and one other necessities or luxuries. Money, from the start, had been the wound in this marriage, a poisoned and poisonous wound. I suppose it is because I suffered so much from it myself, from knowing too much about my mother's sleepless nights of anxiety about bills, that I myself am quite irresponsible (at least by my father's standards) about money. I believe it must flow through me as food does, be spent as it is earned, be given away, be turned into flowers and books and beautiful things, be given to people who are creators or in need, never be counted except as what it is—a counter against more life of one kind or another. It must remain convertible, not allowed to lie fallow. Probably I talk too much about it like someone who has been brought up repressed about sex and tells risqué jokes as a sign of freedom.

The tropical dank wet weather goes on and on, temperature between seventy and eighty. I have to keep a fan going as I write because of the humidity. It is sad because X comes today and I had hoped we could take my rubber boat and go for a swim. I never swim alone. It is a holiday feeling to go trundling off to one of the lakes with the boat.

I do not feel quite knit together, rather at a loose end. Such idleness lately! Why not a holiday? But I never get any sense of accomplishment if I have done nothing but housework, partly because it is never "done" once and for all. Lately it seems as though I were always running to get through these chores to the real things.

August 4th

PUNCH IS DEAD. I have just buried him under the white rosebush by the barn.

He has been such a cheerful companion for two and a half years since I brought him back one February day from the five-and-ten, feeling I must have some presence in the house; it was too lonely while the cats were with Judy in Cambridge in winter. He was a reason for getting up, so happy to be uncovered, greeting daylight with screams of joy, and flying at once to the window sill, then down to a perch outside the cage where he could admire himself in a mirror I had attached to a windowpane.

But for several weeks he had had a tumor over one eye. Four visits to the vet. Each time I held him, pulsing in my hand, while the tumor was cut away. Each time I felt sure he would recover. But this morning after the operation, gruesome and bloody, he lay down in the carrying cage and he was dead when I got home.

Now I have buried him and put his cage and toys away in the attic. That corner of the cosy room looks terribly empty. How much atmosphere he displaced . . . no larger than my hand, cocking his head when I passed by, making sweet murmurs to himself in the evening when I watched the news, so self-contained, cheerful, and brave! The first time I took him to the vet he was given an injection that crippled one leg so he could not sit on a perch. All morning he tried to crawl up the cage and fell back, crawled up and fell back, while Mildred and I sweated it out, helpless to help him. After two and a half hours of this agonizing struggle, he finally made it! It is not absurd to feel such grief. I am undone. He had given me much joy.

Photo by Eleanor Blair

August 9th

THESE DAYS fly past. Marion Hamilton is here, but there are things I must try to capture before I forget. One of the great seasonal events has been taking place these last days, for the Warners are here haying the big meadow. The first person to arrive was Helen in the teetery old truck, dragging the hay-maker behind her and looking handsome in her plain cotton dress. Sometime later we heard the horses' hoofs on Center Pond Road. Bud brings the two farm horses down each day, a good three miles. His stride matches theirs, and he holds them on a tight rein, so the effect is that of a frieze, the sinewy control of a small man treading firmly behind two huge beasts. They come, my friends, the Warners, every year to turn what has become wilderness back into a spacious orderly view way down to the line of maples at the end of the field. It is difficult, tricky work because of the granite rocks strewn about under the tall grasses. This year they unearthed eleven nests of yellow jackets, a real hazard. No one, thank Heaven, has been stung so far except one of the horses. This is the hornet year, I guess, as they come in cycles.

Bud goes up and down the field, first cutting in big swathes, resting the horses often, man and beast in perfect accord. Then Helen or Doris (third member of the haying trio) get at the raking, sitting high on the seat, pulling a lever as each cycle is completed and the huge swathe gathered up and dropped. By the end of the first afternoon they had put a couple of truckloads into the barn. Beautiful to watch the way tall Helen swings up what looks like a ton on her fork!

After the big work is done, there is still the scything, delicate, precise cutting around rocks and trees, and along the stone walls. I never tire of watching Bud with a scythe, the slow rhythm as the ragged line of goldenrod and black-eyed Susans and tall grasses is slowly cut to leave all airy and trim, and form emerging from chaos once more. I hate to see the flowers go, but on these hot August days the need to have space in which to breathe is paramount.

At noon I take out pitchers of iced tea and cookies and it is good to see the horses standing at rest in the shade, their long flowing tails swishing back and forth against the flies, and the Warners eating lunch on the grass beside them.

How silent it all is compared to what it would be if the job were done by machine—silent, and every gesture beautiful! I think of all the gentle sounds these haying days bring —the Warners' voices, never raised in anger or impatience, the thud of hoods on dirt road, the whisper of a scythe, the rumble of the old truck. "Sweet, especial rural scene"—I am lucky to have had a last glimpse of what will not be seen after I am dead, or even before. For who, nowadays, has either the skill or the patience or the caring to do this kind of job in this way, the standards so high and the work so arduous?

August 16th

IT IS RATHER a joke to be keeping a journal of solitude when I have had none to speak of for weeks! Where has the summer gone? Two or three days ago the change happened, that change in the light, that sudden coolness and clarity that speaks of autumn just around the corner. The garden looks seedy except for a few marvelous lilies, Crimson Emperor, for one. I woke with Robert Frost's poem running through my head, the one that ends,

> I could give all to Time except—except
> What I myself have held. But why declare
> The things forbidden that while the Customs slept
> I have crossed to Safety with? For I am There.
> And what I would not part with I have kept.

There is only one real deprivation, I decided this morning, and that is not to be able to give one's gifts to those one loves most. In the month when X seemed withdrawn what was hardest to handle was the feeling I had that it no longer meant very much to hear me read a poem. The gift turned inward, unable to be given, becomes a heavy burden, even sometimes a kind of poison. It is as though the flow of life were backed up.

Marion Hamilton and I had a full rich week together that held in it two large events of differing kinds. We went to Maine to see the house there, where I plan to move in a year or two. It was only my second sight of it, and the first had been on a cold gray April morning. This second visit took place on a radiant summer day, not too hot, and it was breathtaking to come out of the woods and see before us the golden field, shining and rippling, grassy paths cut through it down to the ocean, brilliant blue and dazzling. Such openness and grandeur!

This time all the windows stood open, as workmen were there, so the house itself welcomed us. As I walked through the empty rooms, I felt this time that I can live happily in them, especially now that I have decided to make my study on the third floor. The first time I had wandered around like a cat trying to find somewhere to curl up, a sheltered place. Nothing is really right for a study except that paneled and eaved room at the top.

The second event was a delightful picnic, the Hillsboro County Democratic picnic, held in Alpine Grove, a stand of tall white pines with trestle tables under them and an open field beyond. McGovern, Birch Bayh, and Jackson were all announced as speakers. We took Laurie Armstrong with us and were all three moved by the democratic process, the whole affair informal and human, the speakers standing (no platform) among the people and then moving out to talk with those sitting at tables. I was struck by how much more truly one can sense the quality of a man under these circumstances than on TV. I wrote Birch Bayh off at once when I saw how aware he was of press and photographers, talking earnestly to animals and children for publicity "takes." McGovern, whose speech was strong and humorous and pulled no punches, obviously cared to listen to what individuals came up to ask or to tell him. He came through as authentic. The other two did not. Jackson rides on John Kennedy's coattails. He has small calculating eyes.

August 27th

I FINALLY had to admit that what I had brushed aside as fatigue was a virus infection, and I have been very low and cross these last days on antibiotics that may heal the infection in my chest but just as surely act as a depressant. I had counted for so long on this week—the first week in ages without a guest—that being unable to work filled me with fury. The garden lies there in wait—I don't like to look out, for there is so much that needs doing. Everything is overgrown, everything needs pruning. The iris must be cut down and separated. The family of wild cats eat omnivorously—four kittens like a sampler of kittens (one tiger, one black, one speckled, one marmalade) and their mother. What will happen to them when winter comes? It is one of those times when the place lies on my heart like a heavy burden and I would like to close the door and steal away to almost anywhere, even a hotel, where I would no longer be responsible for sweeping a floor or getting a meal. Everything is terribly dry. Today, at last, looks like rain. I welcome the gray sky.

Yesterday I had a remarkable letter from C, who has been alone in her *Mas* in Provence for two months. I was rather relieved to read that even she with her infinite resources, including that of religion at its deepest and most fruitful, says this about solitude:

Mon expérience de la grande solitude est comme d'un caractère instable—qui par moments vous fortifie et vous exalte puis bientôt vous abat, vous jette dans un état affamé et altéré, dans une attente continue de ce qui n'arrivera pas—et quel ennui de ce qu'on a à faire pour soi tout seul!—plus que tout: préparer sa nourriture et la manger! Je précise le degré de solitude: pendant un mois la femme de ménage qui vit ici était partie pour une maison de repos. L'homme travaillait loin d'ici toute la journée. Je n'ai pas le téléphone, aucun moyen de locomotion—une voisine aimable que j'avais au bas de la colline est morte—un jeune ménage paysan qui était aimable aussi a déménagé pour un village distant de plusieurs kilomètres. J'ai pris l'habitude de "penser accident" et de sentir la solitude comme la certitude de ne pas être secourue si il m'en arrivait un—D'où l'afflux de quantité d'exemples pour m'illustrer la fragilité de notre fabrication.

My experience of great solitude is that its character is unstable—at times exalts and fortifies then soon beats down, and throws one into a starving and thirsty state, into a sustained waiting for what will not happen ... and what a bore what one has to do for oneself alone!— above all, preparing a meal and eating it! Let me make precise the degree of solitude: during a month the farmer's wife who lived here had gone to a rest home. Her husband worked far away from here all day. I have no telephone, no means of transportation—a kind neighbor at the bottom of the hill has died—a young peasant couple who were also kind have moved to a village some kilometers away. I have acquired the habit of "thinking accidents" and of feeling solitude as the certainty that I shall be without help should I have one— hence the arrival of quantities of examples to illustrate for me the fragility of our fabrication.

This letter spoke to me with great force because I always feel abandoned when I am ill here (although I have a telephone, of course, and dear Mildred across the green). I learned long ago that someone without family must really go to a hospital when even moderately ill; any disease that kept me bedridden for even a short time would require hospitalization. There is no *secours*, but it always comes to me with amazement that this is so. It is partly that being ill has no relation to actual time. There was only one day when I could do nothing except lie around, when even reading was no pleasure and TV made my eyes ache ... but that day felt like an eternity.

C is over eighty and the degree of solitude she describes is far more intense than any I have experienced here. I can always get out and drive somewhere. I have the phone. As Haniel Long says in a poem about "our great fragile cities,"

> To keep on living I could recall the time
> When, if only over the telephones,
> We became lights and went seeking
> One another, and were answered by other lights,
> And invisible people speaking.

And what would I do without the evening news on TV? It is not only that I am passionately concerned about what is going on, but equally that the coming into the house of human faces seems like a necessity when I have been alone here all day.

There is no doubt that solitude is a challenge and to maintain balance within it a precarious business. But I must not forget that, for me, being with people or even with one beloved person for any length of time without solitude is even worse. I lose my center. I feel dispersed, scattered, in pieces. I must have time alone in which to mull over any encounter, and to extract its juice, its essence, to understand what has really happened to me as a consequence of it.

After Marion left, Anne Woodson was here for a few days and these were a good test of our deepening friendship, of a kind of rest we experience together, a lack of tension, that is nourishing. Anne put up her easel in the big room and painted while I worked at revising poems. We met for meals, for quiet talks on the porch, went to bed early, and proved that we can live along side by side very happily and fruitfully.

It was a good time, ending with a day when we drove to Maine and had a first picnic there on the rocky beach. Mary Leigh brought lobsters, salad, wine. I felt wild with joy at the prospect before me in another two years. Each time I see the house I feel more able to "tame" and make it mine. The only thing that frightens me is that it is a bit grand for an old raccoon. How much it will change my ethos remains to be experienced, but at least (on a purely mundane level) it will be marvelous to have space in which to put things away— what I lack most here. But that is not so important, of course, as the magnificent view down that golden meadow to open sea. Thinking about it I feel elation.

August 29th

How LOVELY to go out into the garden after the storm! We had the tail end of a small hurricane, about three inches of rain. The whole world feels clean and fresh. Of course, the garden got a battering, but nothing that cannot be remedied when I have an hour in which to go out and stake up. This morning I picked zinnias and cosmos for the house.

The antibiotic did its work. I feel much better. Energy flows back, although not yet the kind that goes into a poem. But I am enjoying the roller coaster of visits, people for lunch and supper yesterday and a friend coming for Sunday dinner. Yesterday I even cleaned the silver!

For lunch came two young men, with one of whom I have been corresponding for some time. T and J arrived with an armful of flowers and two records, and we had a good long talk before they took me out to lunch, a boon, I must confess, as it meant we could sit by the fire and talk, without my fussing around about food. J wishes to enter a monastic order (both are Catholics) and they have been "shopping around" for a monastery in just the way one hears of people "shopping" for a psychiatrist. Here, with a lifetime commitment involved, it becomes a serious and perilous search. One cannot help wondering, looking at a handsome young man, handsome and intelligent, but not yet knit together, how much of this wish for the contemplative life stems from romanticism, even possibly a kind of narcissism. I can understand better after our talk why the monastic orders have to make it *hard* to enter and *hard* to stay. The vocation must be severely tested, even to the applicant's enduring long periods of doubt and/or dryness before one can be certain it is real.

I plunged in and asked them whether I am wrong to believe that the real things happening in Catholic America are among the orders that go out into the world and follow Christ according to his statement, "What ye have done unto the least of these ye have done unto me." Of course, I think of Sister Mary David, and of Ned O'Gorman, of Dorothy Day . . . and of many others. But J wants to be a monk and T a philosopher. Why must I be slightly suspicious of people who know all the VIPs, who arrive in huge black Mercurys, who are expensively dressed? It is no doubt romantic of me, an unbeliever, to wish the religious to be ascetic. But I do not call myself a Christian because I believe that to do so would require giving up all material things and literally going among the most destitute, the sick, the old, or the deprived children. Simone Weil, though she never made the final step, comes close to what my ideal would be. I gave T the Jacques Cabaud biography of her and wonder what he will think of it. She was *not* charming and she stripped herself of every "advantage" to do what she did, at excruciating cost to her health and to her instinctual being, even to her wish to love and to be loved. T is a man who has proved his power to influence others, thinks of himself always as an instrument for God. This is moving, but rather innocent . . . an innocent kind of pride. I may be unduly influenced by my friendship with another man who wanted to be a priest and fought his way out of one seminary after another . . . I am sure with good reason. Yet the danger is a kind of spiritual arrogance, I fear. In a different way these men remind me of idealistic women who never can stay on committees because they always know best, because the committee is not "pure" enough, because they cannot accept compromise.

Against this I set a passage from Jung which I have re-read many times these last weeks. In a way it is an apologia for the man who does choose to be a contemplative. It opens the way to a justification for such a vocation.

> If you imagine someone who is brave enough to withdraw all his projections, then you get an individual who is conscious of a pretty thick shadow. Such a man has saddled himself with new problems and conflicts.

He has become a serious problem to himself, as he is now unable to say that *they* do this or that, *they* are wrong, and *they* must be fought against. He lives in "The House of Gathering." Such a man knows that whatever is wrong in the world is in himself, and if he only learns to deal with his own shadow he has done something real for the world. He has succeeded in shouldering at least an infinitesimal part of the gigantic, unsolved social problems of our day.

September 11th

I AM IN PURGATORY because I have no days alone and have not had for too long a space. But there have been some marvelous happenings, so let me dwell on them. Two nights ago, after a rather frantic day, Judy and I (she is here for a week) went out to walk around the green in the dark and found ourselves under the most brilliant starry sky I have seen in weeks. Suddenly the moist air had cleared. The Milky Way streamed across over our heads and one huge bright planet stood over the hill. But the loveliest thing was to look up at stars shining through the leaves, a rare sight because summer nights do not often have such clarity. I associate a sky like this with autumn after the leaves have gone.

I have been much moved to be with Judy again after two months when we were not able to meet. I begin to understand that she is very quietly realizing her deep self all these days when she often seems absent and is increasingly forget- ful of mundane matters; but under them her spirit shines with a quiet, strong flame. And though she is in some ways leading a deprived life since her retirement, she says almost every day, "I have been so lucky," and rejoices in all she has had. It is true that she has had behind her a family tradition of imaginative loving-kindness. I am deeply impressed by the goodness of Judy's family, and the way they help one another, discreetly, without being intrusive. It is appalling to think how rare simple loving-kindness has become.

We celebrated Judy's seventy-third birthday this week. I stuffed a chicken and Laurie came to share it with us. Judy and I have been friends for nearly thirty years.

September 15th

BECAUSE OF various encounters recently I am haunted by Basil de Selincourt's remark to me years ago, "You Americans give too much." How unconscious we are, often, that giving may actually be asking, asking at the very least for attention. I am sure I err in this way myself. This kind of giving for self- ish reasons often ends in frustration and even in recrimina- tion: "I have given you so much. Why don't you answer or respond?" which is to say, "When I love you so much, why can't you love me?" There are times lately when I dream only of disappearing, taking another name, settling in to some place where no one would recognize me or care. I suffer because I know too much about the people who project their needs onto me (often people I have never seen who regard me as an intimate friend and who pour out their lives, taking it for granted that I must care). I have been there myself, and so I too give too much. I create the illusion of caring out of compassion and out of guilt—and that only makes matters worse. For then the reckoning comes—the hurt question, "Why did you answer at all if you didn't mean to take me into your life?"

Many years ago I had a vivid dream after Virginia Woolf's suicide. I dreamt that I saw her walking in the streets of a provincial town, unrecognized, unknown, and somehow guessed that she had not committed suicide at all, but had decided that she had to disappear, go under as her famous self, and start again.

Last night I skimmed through the new edition of *The Bridge of Years* just to see how it tasted now after twenty-five years. Not too bad, although I would not write like that now. I have pared my style down. It is less obviously "poetic" these days. I was struck by this statement made by Paul: "It takes a long time, all one's life, to learn to love one person well—with enough distance, with enough humility, he thought."

Yesterday Judy and I talked about this very thing in relation to Z, who has been such a trial these last days. Perhaps the greatest gift we can give to another human being is detachment. Attachment, even that which imagines it is selfless, *always* lays some burden on the other person. How to learn to love in such a light, airy way that there is no burden? Jean Dominique achieved it at the end of her life, and certainly Edith Kennedy many years ago gave me intimations of this difficult skill by the way she handled diverse friends, and the passionate attachments she aroused.

Is it a flaw in me that attracts passionate attachments that I cannot handle and do not want? It may be that Basil was right. Perhaps I give too much and in the wrong way. But it is partly because I have gone in need so often—the need for what those I loved would not or could not give— that I have made a kind of resolve to try always to answer. Rebecca West says, "Surely in each human being there is both a hungry naked outcast and a Sister of Charity, desolate without those whom she can feed and clothe and shelter, and these cannot minister to each other. That is the rule which has been put in to make it more difficult. They must find a stranger outside the skin to whose Sister of Charity the outcast can offer his rose, to whose outcast, the Sister of Charity can offer her pity."

The strange effect of all these "lovers" is to make me feel not richer, but impoverished and mean, and it is then I who ask the childish questions, "Haven't I given you enough? Can't you leave me in peace to do my work?" The frustration grows in me and finally I wreck whatever I have done by an outburst of anger that may be cruel.

I have seen in a friend of mine who is a psychiatrist a kind of passive waiting, not open, a secret person, not giving herself away, simply the passive receptacle of feeling. I can see her hands lying quite still in her lap as she listens.

September 16th

I AM STILL ruffled and badgered by the whole problem of Z and cannot get it out of my head. I know from my own experience that, once the imagination crystallizes (to use the Stendhalian image) around another human being, it is a *fait accompli*. The imagination then sustains itself on very little in the way of response, and the rewards may be great to the person who feels so intensely. That being so, why not give what one can?

I have seen Z exactly three times in three years, but I have tried to be as supportive as I can from a distance, tried to be a nondestructive muse for her gifts as a poet. But the gift has become suspect, I suppose, because I have the eerie feeling when I read Z's poems that I am being echoed. I might have written them myself. And from there I have come to see this demanding, insatiable person who must always explain herself in letters that spill over into verbalism, single-spaced, endless pages of them, as a grotesque cartoon of me. My faults too have been those of excess; I too have made emotional demands without being aware of what I was asking; I too have imagined that I was giving when I was battering at someone for attention. And it is just because I am aware of this that I am both kind and constantly alarmed and upset by a presence in my life that I did not want, that has imposed itself willy-nilly, and that finally creates repulsion because in it I must face my own faults magnified and distorted. I have learned some measure and discipline when it comes to dealing with words. The more articulate one is, the more dangerous words become. It is necessary to be as exact and as circumspect as possible in order to tell the truth. But Z—so much younger than I—has not learned this discipline. She spills over and the effect is that of a lush flower that has gone to seed before it has come into its form, an effect of waste, not of richness.

I am haunted, of course, by the remark made to me by a psychiatrist whom I saw briefly many years ago about another such problem. She had seen me teaching at Breadloaf at the Writers' Conference, and she said, "People want to become you and when they find they cannot, they want to kill you." In a quite irrational way I fear Z. I fear her because I cannot take her into my life and even at a distance she eats up time and energy I do not really have to give. Where will it end?

I know that after a dispersed and uncentering summer I must get back to my own center and get back to work. Otherwise I begin to feel like a disposal unit that, if filled too full, gets stuck and can no longer dispose of anything. The physical symptom is nausea in this machine, myself. I want to throw up what I am asked to contain and to digest.

Z has been the background of these last days. The foreground is the wild cat. She had four delightful kittens a few weeks old, but was herself pregnant again. I could not touch her or catch her or get anywhere near her. I took saucers of milk and food out to the whole family and set them under a bush in the garden. In two months there will be more kittens, and by then these four will be nearly grown and begin producing. I woke in the middle of one night with a vision of hundreds of cats and kittens, multiplying indefinitely ... a nightmare. So I had to come to a decision, a hard one, and called the Humane Society. They came five days ago and managed to catch one of the full-grown orange sons, but of course the wild mother was off and away at once. I talked the problem over with the gentle kind man who had come, and he suggested leaving a large cage on the porch for a few days and gradually taming the cat and kittens to eat inside it. Then on some terrible morning I was to close the door and call him to come to fetch them. Every morning since then I have wakened at five, feeling doom ahead, and once I did manage to get the whole family inside the cage. But that, by mischance, was the man's day off, so I had to let them go without closing the door. It was all to do again. Yesterday the wild cat looked at me in a terrible way, her lip half lifted in fear. All winter I have met her steady fascinated gaze, all winter have been building trust between us, and now I was to betray it. She was very hungry and finally did go in with the orange kitten and I managed to snap the cage door fast.

At once she and the kitten battered themselves against it, up and down from roof to floor, in a paroxysm of terror. I fled into the house in despair. When I phoned the Humane Society the man was here in an hour and took them away. How to live with what I have done? I had to do it. But I shall carry it with me, buried somewhere, until I die. I betrayed an animal that trusted me.

But if I shall never forget the wild cat I shall also never forget the kindness of that gentle man. He saw how upset I was and with perfect dignity and truth tried to reassure me. He said that for the mother the end would be quick, and promised to try to find a home for her kitten. I cannot go through this trauma again and will keep the three remaining kittens, tame them and in time have them neutered. I have named them—the black one Pierrot, the speckled one Bramble, and the tiger Bel-Gazou. By winter perhaps I can get them to come in to sleep on my bed.

September 30th

I HAVE BEEN silent while the great autumn light begins, a time of change in the inner world. We have been spared killing frost so far, but I have wakened twice to a silver meadow. Because the picking garden is close to the house and sheltered, there are still zinnias and cosmos to pick, though they fade quickly indoors. The glory now is the autumn crocuses, brilliant along the front borders with lavender asters above them, a patch of beauty in the otherwise destitute garden. The long sequence of flowers that began with a clump of snowdrops by the granite step in April is almost at an end. But of course now light moves upward from the flower borders to the leaves overhead—saffron yellow of the beeches, vermilion and orange of the maples, wave on wave of massed translucent color, the stained-glass days against a brilliant blue sky.

All summer I have been wavering before the decision that has been slowly ripening in me that the time has come to break away from X. This journal began a year ago with depression, with much self-questioning about my dangerous and destructive angers, with the hope that self-examination would help me to change. I made great efforts at control and sometimes I succeeded. But there were things between X and me that could not be solved, a clash not only of temperaments but of fundamental values, the vision of life itself. Possibly each of us at nearly sixty suffers from professional deformation, the other side of our power as individuals. The reasons for anger were often childish or irrelevant and the anger left us always dismayed by our failure toward each other, but the fact is that neither of us could command the necessary tolerance. Passionate love has nothing to do with that. In the first year it was enough, overwhelmingly good and fruitful, but there was no foundation of understanding on another level, and no time to make one. In the end we could not give each other our best, and that was tragic. Each of us, no doubt, felt attacked, misunderstood. We treated each other badly.

After the break my first feeling was relief. But a few days later I became really ill, as though something as essential as blood were flowing out of me. Nausea . . . tears.

I begin to have intimations, now, of a return to some deep self that has been too absorbed and too battered to function for a long time. That self tells me that I was meant to live alone, meant to write the poems for others—poems that seldom in my life have reached the one person for whom they were intended.

Yesterday I got the manuscript of *A Durable Fire* off to Norton. When I began writing those poems I had had the dream that I would celebrate my sixtieth birthday with a book of joys, a book speaking of fulfillment and happiness. But on the final re-reading I saw clearly that it is an elegiac book and that the seeds of parting were in it from the beginning. This is where poetry is so mysterious, the work more mature than the writer of it, always the messenger of growth. So perhaps we write toward what we will become from where we are. The book is less and more than I had imagined it might be. But it could not have been written without all that X gave me, nor, for that matter, without what was lacking between us.

This is the first "Nelson day" for weeks, a day when I can stay home, work at my desk in peace, no appointment looming ahead, a day when I can rest after work, and garden in the afternoon. Once more the house and I are alone.

FINIS